SECRET LEXINGTON

A Guide to the Weird, Wonderful, and Obscure

Fiona Young-Brown

Reedy Press
PO Box 5131
St. Louis, MO 63139
reedypress.com

Library of Congress Control Number: 2025936865
ISBN: 9781681066141

Design by Jill Halpin

Unless otherwise indicated, all photos are courtesy of the author or in the public domain.

We (the publisher and the author) have done our best to provide the most accurate information available when this book was completed. However, we make no warranty, guarantee, or promise about the accuracy, completeness, or currency of the information provided, and we expressly disclaim all warranties, express or implied. Please note that attractions, company names, addresses, websites, and phone numbers are subject to change or closure, and this is outside of our control. We are not responsible for any loss, damage, injury, or inconvenience that may occur due to the use of this book. When exploring new destinations, please do your homework before you go. You are responsible for your own safety and health when using this book.

Printed in the United States of America
25 26 27 28 29   5 4 3 2 1

For Nic,
without whom I would never have found Lexington

The Vogt Reel House features some striking historic architecture.

ACKNOWLEDGMENTS

Although writing is a solitary process, the preparation and collection of information is most definitely a team effort.

Thanks go out to the many local businesses, organizations, and people who have helped with this book. You answered my many questions, shared images, provided tours (sometimes at odd hours), and offered valuable behind-the-scenes info. You were all an essential part of this book.

The Lexington Writer's Room provides a physical space to work and a community of other writers who can offer encouragement. I am so pleased to have found such a wonderful bunch of creatives.

Thanks to my husband, Nic, for his patience and his help with photos and visiting various spots. Although they cannot read this, thank you to my dogs, Milo and Loki, for trying to understand why I couldn't play ball all the time and for knowing that sometimes a good walk can clear the mind.

Last but not least, if I have forgotten anyone important, I humbly apologize and ask you to know that I am deeply appreciative.

The Valley View Ferry is the oldest continually operating business in Kentucky.

CONTENTS

For some spring color, head to the Lexington Cemetery to enjoy the cherry blossoms. Courtesy Mary L. Nichols

INTRODUCTION

How do you decide what is secret? Is it something that only the locals know? Is it something that only a handful of people know? That was just one of the challenges facing me with this book. I moved to Lexington in 2001. Surely that was enough time to uncover some of the city's secrets?

For more guidance, I looked to the subtitle: the Weird, Wonderful, and Obscure. Well, Lexington has its fair share of weird and obscure. Those are precisely the things that make it so wonderful.

Why does part of town smell like peanuts on a still day? Why was there an annual bed race (sadly no more) dedicated to a local madam? And who buries someone beneath the stairs? Surely, if I could answer these odd questions, more would follow.

And they did. With each visit to a different location around town, I noticed a common remark: "Have you heard about . . . ?" I would then be regaled with further weirdness, some of which I already knew, and some that went down in the notebook to explore.

This is by no means an exhaustive list of all that is weird, wonderful, and obscure in Lexington. What's obscure to one reader might be obvious to another. Instead, I present 84 vignettes looking at some of the history, people, and places that have made this city so wonderful.

May you discover and embrace something new in *Secret Lexington.*

I DREAM OF MONKEYS

Where does a global fairytale begin?

Most visitors to Lexington know about the various horse murals around town, and of course the giant technicolor Abraham Lincoln that adorns a wall near the bus station. What they may not know is that the streets of Lexington are the unlikely starting point for a magical fairytale that spans several continents. German artistic duo Herakut transformed two ordinary walls into the opening chapters of their "Giant Storybook Series."

Herakut is comprised of Jasmin Siddiqui ("Hera") and Falk Lehmann ("Akut"). Siddiqui is a classically trained artist while Lehmann is self-taught. Together, they create distinctive works that

THE GIANT STORYBOOK SERIES

WHAT: The first two panels in a set of fantasy murals that circle the world

WHERE: 153 Market St. and 574 N Limestone St.

COST: Free

PRO TIP: VisitLex has created a mural challenge to encourage visitors to seek out and learn about the city's extensive street art collection.

The first mural in the series introduces us to Lily and her two monkey companions.

The second fairytale mural depicts the goddess of dreams holding two baby giants in her hand.

are both whimsical and hyper-realistic.

The first, "Lily and the Silly Monkeys," was painted in 2012 and introduced Lily, the series' young protagonist. With Herakut's signature blend of whimsical characters and photorealistic elements, the mural depicts Lily's playful encounter with two mischievous monkeys. And so the story begins, inviting passersby into a world where imagination rules.

The second installment, "Where Dreams Come From," expands the fairytale universe. Here, we meet Lily's brother, Jay, along with two gentle giants who serve as guardians of childhood wonder. The mural suggests that dreams originate not from sleep but from open-eyed curiosity about the world—a theme that resonates throughout Herakut's work.

Their Lexington murals mark the beginning of a global narrative, and are part of Lexington's ever-expanding collection of striking public artworks.

As the first chapters in what promises to be an expansive international fairytale, these murals do more than beautify buildings—they invite the community to become part of a story still being written, one wall at a time.

Other installments of the Giant Storybook Series can be found in various locations throughout the US, Canada, and Europe, as well as Australia and Nepal.

MYSTERIOUS MOUNDS

Who were the earliest people in Lexington?

The rolling hills of the Bluegrass Region were populated long before the European settlers arrived. The Cherokee, Shawnee, and Chickasaw people were all indigenous to the area. But who was here before them? That was the question William Snyder Webb set out to answer.

When the University of Kentucky set up its anthropology and archaeology department in 1926, it invited Webb to be the department chair. Although a physicist by training, he had developed a strong interest in Native American history while working in the Oklahoma Territory.

Webb oversaw archaeological excavations at a number of sites in the Kentucky–Ohio region, including the Mount Horeb Earthworks Complex. The earthworks, which lie on the banks of North Elkhorn Creek, are the oldest known inhabited site in the state. It had been first "discovered" in the early 19th century but was not explored in depth until 1939, when the Works Progress Administration (WPA) included it in their depression-relief plans.

The central mound is about 32 meters wide. Around it is a ditch, approximately four meters wide, and enclosing it all is a dirt embankment. In total, it is roughly 90 meters in diameter.

The earthwork was constructed by the Adena people, who lived in the Bluegrass between 500 BCE and 300 CE. Archaeologists still know little about their way of life, but excavations at Mount Horeb suggest they used the mound for ceremonial purposes.

More than 19,000 archaeological sites have been cataloged in Kentucky; the oldest date to the Paleo-Indian period, some 11,000 years ago.

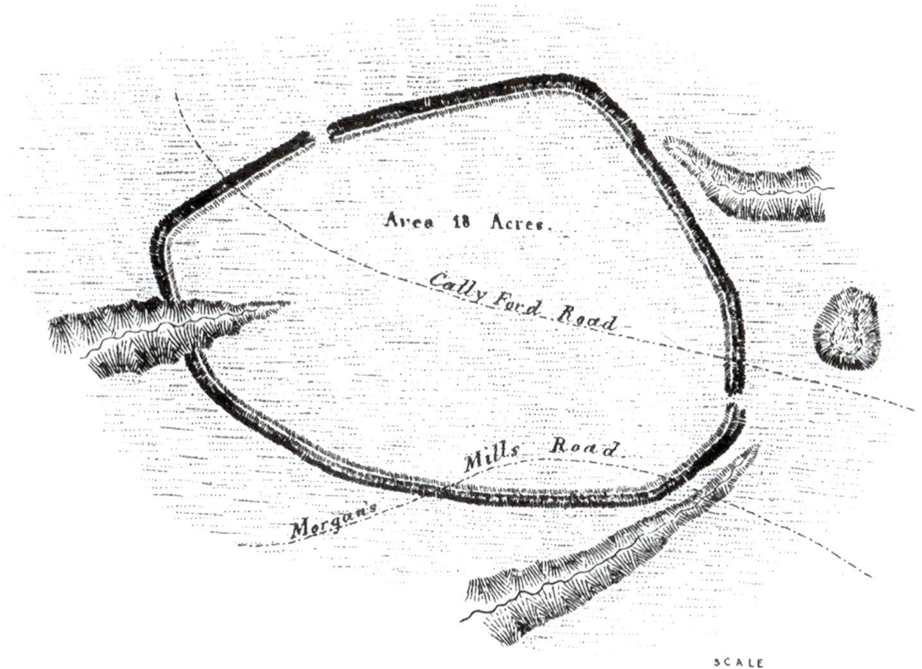

Above: *This 1848 diagram by Ephraim George Squier and Edwin Hamilton Davis maps one of the mounds at Mount Horeb.*

Left: *Entry to the Adena Park is strictly forbidden without permission.*

Several smaller mounds, also attributed to the Adena, can be seen from the Mount Horeb site.

The Mount Horeb Earthworks Complex is owned by the University of Kentucky and is open only to those with express permission.

MOUNT HOREB EARTHWORKS COMPLEX

WHAT: Pre-Columbian mounds

WHERE: 4470 Mt. Horeb Pike

COST: Free to look through the locked entry gate

PRO TIP: Other mounds around Lexington are on Lemons Mill Road and Clay Avenue.

BUILDING A FAIRYTALE

Is this romantic landmark really a case of happily ever after?

There was one thing on the lips of people throughout Lexington on the morning of May 11, 2004. The castle had burned. Flames could be seen from miles away, the smoke even further. At first, people thought the cause may have been a lightning strike to a turret. Later, firefighters concluded that arson was more likely. Either way, it seemed as though the mysterious building may never be finished.

But why was there a castle in the middle of Kentucky, anyway?

The eye-catching structure, technically not in Lexington but just across the county line, was a point of interest for both locals and visitors who would pull off the road to take photos. Few knew of the broken love story behind it.

In 1969, Rex Martin began building a castle for his wife, Caroline. She had been entranced by the castles of Europe on their honeymoon, and so he was determined to give her something equally majestic.

THE KENTUCKY CASTLE

WHAT: Hotel, restaurant, and event space

WHERE: 230 Pisgah Pike, Versailles

COST: Tours are available for a fee. Dining and room options are more.

PRO TIP: Tour tickets go on sale one month in advance.

Building such a castle took time, and when the Martins divorced in 1975, all work drew to a halt. Only half-finished, it lay abandoned for close to 30 years, a curiosity for passers-by.

In 2003, Martin died, and an attorney, Thomas Post, bought the property, immediately beginning renovations. Barely one year later, the fateful fire destroyed almost everything. Undeterred, Post rebuilt, and the Castle Post opened as an exclusive bed-and-breakfast in 2007.

In 2017, the property was sold again and renamed The Kentucky Castle. The site is used as a hotel, farm-to-table

Top: *The castle rose from romantic beginnings that it continues to honor as a wedding venue. Courtesy The Kentucky Castle*

Bottom: *The castle is an eye-catching landmark on the road into Lexington. Courtesy The Kentucky Castle*

restaurant, and wedding venue. Guests can stay in one of the tower suites, relax in the spa, enjoy a dinner with produce grown on-site, or indulge their princess fantasies at one of the seasonal balls.

Architectural Digest magazine named The Kentucky Castle the most beautiful hotel in the state and one of the most beautiful castles in the world to sleep in.

BIG BLUE

What's the tallest building in Lexington?

If you're visiting anywhere new, it's always helpful to have that one landmark that serves as a reminder of where you are—that place that, when you see it on the horizon, you know which way to go.

In Lexington, that is the Lexington Financial Center. At 410 feet (125 meters) in height, it is the tallest building in the city.

It is commonly reported to have 31 stories, even on the architect's website. In fact, it has 30. There is no 13th floor, which explains why the elevator shows 31.

The skyscraper was built in 1987. It houses several businesses, including an architect's office, a law practice, an insurance company, and two banks.

The observation deck is closed to the public. Several restaurants and bars in downtown Lexington offer good rooftop viewing and let you see Big Blue.

Big Blue stands out above the city skyline. Courtesy Boyd Shearer, UK Department of Geography

So what makes it stand out? Its octagonal shape? Its trapezoid roof? How about its eye-catching blue-glass exterior? The entire building is cased in tinted glass that reflects the downtown cityscape.

The tower is a popular local landmark, but it's also been conquered by a few intrepid souls in the name of charity. In 2013, 308 people climbed 51 flights of stairs (that's 1,134 steps) at the Lexington Financial Center and the neighboring Central Bank Building as part of the Urban Mountain Challenge. Later the same year, more than 100 people rappelled down the side of the building in the Brave the Blue Challenge.

To the locals, it goes by many names: "Big Blue," "the 5/3 Building" (for one of the banks based there), or even "the Big Blue Trashcan" on account of its distinctive shape. Whatever you call it, it stands as a beacon to guide you downtown. Or, if you're flying into the Bluegrass, a sign that you've arrived.

LEXINGTON FINANCIAL CENTER

WHAT: The world's largest building (at least that's what some locals call it)

WHERE: 250 W Main St.

COST: Free, but you may not be allowed in unless visiting one of the on-site offices

PRO TIP: Photograph it early in the morning or close to dusk.

GO MEDIEVAL

Where can you sleep like a Lannister?

Walking down Lexington's Third Street is a step back in time. The old houses you'll see there, with their distinctive towers and verandas, were once home to some of the city's most well-to-do families. One can't help but wonder what they would have looked like inside.

Then you come to a few smaller but equally aged houses, many of them now used as office space. And then you pass a house built in the 1800s but now altered to be an apartment building. In truth, it seems rather nondescript.

At least from the outside.

Your first clue that this apartment is a little out of the ordinary is the wrought-iron door handle as you enter. But that is nothing compared to what awaits you inside.

Owner Wayne Ebersohl has spared no expense in designing this unique place. The theme? Television's popular *Game of Thrones* series. George R. R. Martin's series of novels was transformed into a hugely popular television series that ran for eight seasons from 2011 to 2019. Now fans can enter their own little piece of Westeros, right here in central Kentucky.

An elaborate shield accompanied by battle axes and other weaponry hangs above the fireplace. All were hand-forged by Ukrainian blacksmiths. A giant four-poster bed is draped with furs, guaranteed to keep you warm on the coldest of nights. There's even a dungeon beneath. And of course, there must be dragons! A trio of eggs waits to hatch on the hearth.

The ornate wooden mantel was hand-carved from downed ash trees from the grounds of Spindletop Hall, a private club near the Kentucky Horse Park.

Top: *Care has been taken to pay homage to the George R. R. Martin series down to the tiniest details. Courtesy Bo Stamper*

Bottom: *From the street, there is no clue that a medieval adventure awaits behind closed doors. Courtesy Bo Stamper*

SLEEPING MEDIEVAL STYLE

WHAT: *Game of Thrones*–themed Air BnB

WHERE: Third St. (address provided to guests)

COST: Nightly rates vary plus fees

PRO TIP: Get up early for fresh beignets at Doodles, just a few hundred yards away.

The attention to detail is quite breathtaking. Even if you have not watched the television show or read the books, this is a place that is hard to forget.

RAISE A GLASS

What secret lies within this tiny bookstore?

The unassuming passer-by will barely notice this tiny building on a side street near downtown Lexington. There is no signage, no parking lot, no indication of anything out of the ordinary. Even if a passer-by were to step inside, they would see a tiny room packed with old books from floor to ceiling.

The only clue is a tiny sign encouraging visitors to ring the bell. Ring it and wait to see if someone lets you in.

Welcome to Constitution Rare & Antique Books, the bookstore that's really a speakeasy.

Hidden away behind a faux-bookstore frontage is an exclusive cocktail bar with room for just 40 customers. Reminiscent of a bygone era, its dark-wooded furnishings take you back in time to the Roaring Twenties. Step inside and take a seat at the bar or a table in the cozy back room, reached via a narrow hallway.

If you are lucky enough to be seated at the bar, you can watch the magic happen as the bartenders whisk up all manner of libations, both classic and updated with Constitution's unique twist. They'll also share stories about each drink and the genius behind their creation.

As your taste buds are tickled and you soak up the atmosphere, you may well find yourself expressing gratitude for the bourbon distilleries that were able to remain open during Prohibition, as well as those that have come since.

CONSTITUTION

WHAT: Prohibition-style cocktail bar

WHERE: 109 Constitution St.

COST: Cocktail prices vary.

PRO TIP: Constitution opens at 4 p.m., Wednesday through Sunday. Reservations are recommended.

Top: *Every drink is expertly prepared by Constitution's bartenders. Courtesy Kelly Hieronymous and Constitution*

Bottom Left: *A humble bookstore. Or is it? Courtesy Nic Brown*

Bottom Right: *As with old speakeasies, a disguised entry reveals a hidden bar.*

The bar's specialty is the Jane Eyre, a deliciously delicate combination of Earl Grey–infused gin, cherry blossom syrup, blueberry puree, lime, and sparkling wine.

BRING THE JELLY

Why does Lexington smell like peanut butter?

As you walk around certain parts of Lexington, you may catch a certain aroma in the air. It's not a permanent thing. It comes and goes with the wind. Once your nose catches it, you'll be asking yourself, "What's that smell?"

Chances are you have caught a whiff of the tons of roasted peanuts that are about to become peanut butter at the Lexington Jif plant.

Everyone knows various stories about the origin of peanut butter, from the Aztecs to George Washington Carver. Lexington owes its peanut butter manufacturing roots to local businessman W. T. Young. In 1946, he launched a food company bearing his name. One of its products was Big Top peanut butter. In 1955, Young sold his company to Procter & Gamble. After a few years of rebranding, Jif peanut butter was launched in both creamy and crunchy varieties. An extra crunchy version was launched in 1976.

Procter & Gamble sold the Jif company to J.M. Smucker in 2002, creating the perfect peanut butter and jelly partnership.

J.M. SMUCKER FACTORY

WHAT: The world's largest peanut butter factory

WHERE: 767 Winchester Rd.

COST: Free sniffs

PRO TIP: You can't tour the factory, but there are lots of places to enjoy a peanut butter burger followed by some peanut butter pie.

The main library on the University of Kentucky campus was named in honor of William T. Young after he donated $5 million to the construction project in 1994.

Today Jif is the most popular peanut butter in US grocery stores, accounting for more than 30 percent of all peanut butter purchases. A large portion of that is made right here in Lexington at the Winchester Road factory. (Despite common claims that it is all made in Lexington, some is made at a plant in Tennessee).

In what some might consider true Willy Wonka style, the factory is notoriously secretive. Public tours are not allowed, and few get to see the magic behind the gates. However, that enticing aroma may strike at any time, so don't forget the jelly!

Top: *You might catch the aroma from the world's largest peanut butter manufacturing plant on Winchester Road.*

Left: *Crunchy, creamy, or extra crunchy—which do you prefer? Courtesy Jif*

A POLITICAL HAIRBALL

Is this the oddest museum in Kentucky?

If you lived in Lexington in the early 19th century and wanted to become a doctor, you could head east for your education in Massachusetts, Philadelphia, or New York, or you could stay right here and go to Transylvania University (locally known as Transy). The school made history by having the first medical school west of the Allegheny Mountains.

For a while, it was one of the nation's top medical schools. However, in 1859, the medical department closed its doors.

That closure has since contributed to one of the strangest museums in the state, perhaps even the country. The school's teaching tools and apparatus were all put into storage, and today they are all part of the Moosnick Medical and Science Museum.

The Moosnick is named for Dr. Monroe Moosnick, a Transy graduate and chemistry professor who served as the collection's curator for more than 40 years.

The collection consists of approximately 1,000 uncatalogued artifacts, including a large number of medical instruments brought over from London and Paris in the 1820s. There are also hundreds of anatomical models and bones, plus some more unusual artifacts. If you're keen to see remnants of the 1876 Kentucky Meat Shower, a plaster model of Siamese Twins, or the Wax Venus (a life-size anatomical figure), the Moosnick is the place to go.

The oddest item in the collection may be a 14-inch hairball or bezoar. Donated by Abraham Lincoln's brother-in-law, it would once have been used as an antidote for poison.

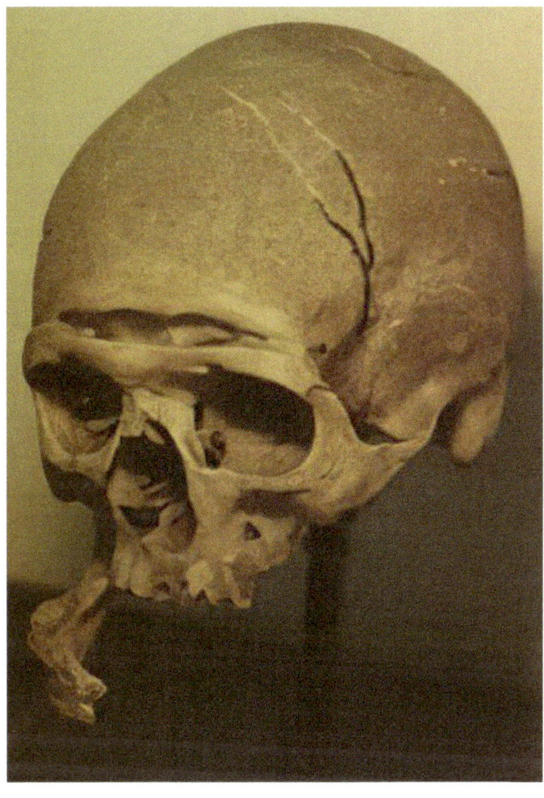

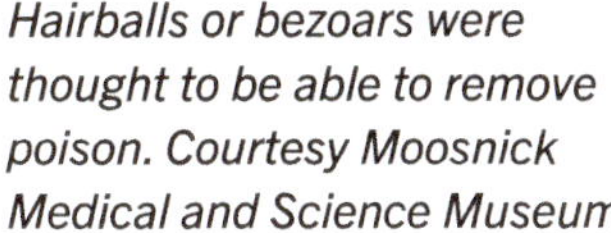

Hairballs or bezoars were thought to be able to remove poison. Courtesy Moosnick Medical and Science Museum

The museum contains a vast collection of historic medical and teaching materials. Courtesy Moosnick Medical and Science Museum

The Moosnick Museum is unusual in that it has no set location. Plans to build a permanent home have yet to materialize. Since the artifacts are stored around campus, they are viewable only by arrangement with the current curator, Dr. Jamie Day.

MOOSNICK MEDICAL AND SCIENCE MUSEUM

WHAT: Collection of scientific and medical artifacts

WHERE: Transylvania University

COST: Free

PRO TIP: "Researchers and the curious" are welcome to arrange a time to visit.

PLAY BALL

Where can you watch an old-timey baseball game?

Did you know that Lexington has two baseball teams?

Most people know about the Lexington Legends, the professional team based at Legends Field. But for a change of pace, how about a leisurely Sunday afternoon sitting in the sun and watching the men play like it's 1869?

The Bluegrass Barons are the state's only vintage base ball team. Note that even the spelling of the sport is vintage.

Ben "Pops" Clouse spent more than 30 years playing softball before retiring. His introduction to vintage base ball was a game between two out-of-state teams at Lexington's Waveland State Historic Site. He was immediately intrigued and set about forming a local team.

How does vintage base ball differ from the modern game? For starters, there are no gloves, helmets, or shin guards, and pitches are underhanded. Catching the ball barehanded takes considerable skill. The ball is different, as are the outfits. But there are also differences in the rules. For instance, the arbiter

BLUEGRASS BARONS

WHAT: 1869-rules baseball team

WHERE: Waveland State Historic Site, 225 Waveland Museum Ln.

COST: All home games are free.

PRO TIP: Bring a picnic and lawn chairs or a blanket.

The 1869 rules predate the first professional baseball league. The National Association of Professional Base Ball Players was founded in 1871. It was later replaced by the National League and, eventually, Major League Baseball.

Above: *The Bluegrass Barons strive for historical accuracy from outfits to rules. Courtesy Bluegrass Barons*

Right: *Up to bat against the Mariah Hill Yanks. Courtesy Bluegrass Barons*

(umpire) rarely calls a strike, and there is no running through first base.

The rules can get rather complicated at times because the Barons play by 1869 rules, but some of the other teams use early 1860 rules. (There's a difference.) If there's a dispute about a ruling, then it's time for the players to reach a "gentleman's agreement," as they would have done in the 19th century.

The Bluegrass Barons played their first game in 2016 and have been gaining a following ever since. They play as many as 30 games a season against teams from the surrounding states and have a record of 138 wins in 214 games. The season runs from March to October, with regular games in Lexington.

HAIL THE KING

Who proved himself a hero during the cholera epidemic?

In 1833, Lexington was a small but growing town, the "Athens of the West." There was a successful medical school at Transylvania University, and prominent local families had high hopes for the town's future.

Then disaster struck.

That summer, cholera came to town. Unknown to doctors at the time, the disease spread through contaminated water. The Town Branch, which ran through the center of town, was overflowing after heavy rains. Privies and outhouses overflowed, and the excess water washed the waste back into the drinking supply. Once people contracted the disease, there was little hope.

The bodies began to pile up so quickly that there was no one to bury them. Until King Solomon stepped in to help.

William "King" Solomon was once a local construction worker. But in the decades leading up to the cholera outbreak his love of alcohol had won over, and he was known to all as the local drunk. In 1833, after an arrest for drunkenness and

The townspeople of Lexington came forward to fund a headstone for Solomon. Courtesy Nic Brown

The only known portrait of King Solomon. Courtesy Junior League of Lexington

TOMB OF WILLIAM "KING" SOLOMON AT LEXINGTON CEMETERY

WHAT: Resting place of a local hero

WHERE: 833 W Main St.

COST: Free

PRO TIP: A portrait of Solomon hangs in the Bodley-Bullock House.

vagrancy, he was sold on the town auction block. His buyer was a free black woman, Aunt Charlotte.

Solomon's years of digging ditches had made him strong, and when the cholera epidemic hit the town, he set to work, burying the victims of the epidemic. His preference for whiskey over water probably saved him from contracting cholera.

Eventually, an estimated 500 of the town's 6,000-strong population succumbed to the disease. As for Solomon, he lived to the ripe old age of 79. When he died in 1854, he was buried in the Lexington Cemetery where he had laid so many others to rest. The preacher at his funeral said he had "drunk whiskey enough to float a man-o-war." In 1908, the townspeople bought a monument for him.

Solomon claimed to have known another local hero, Henry Clay, during his childhood in Virginia. Clay's much larger tomb is nearby.

THE MOSTEST HOSS

Why was this sporting champion's grave relocated?

Of all the thoroughbreds born and raised in central Kentucky, only a few go on to be champion racehorses. Fewer still become legends.

Described by the National Museum of Racing and Hall of Fame as "an equine freight train," Man o' War had the perfect combination of speed and power. Some would argue there has never been another horse like him.

THE EQUINE FREIGHT TRAIN

WHAT: The burial spot of racehorse Man o' War

WHERE: The Kentucky Horse Park, 4058 Iron Works Pike

COST: Free to visit the grave. There is an admission fee to visit the rest of the Kentucky Horse Park. The park is closed Mondays and Tuesdays.

PRO TIP: See other retired racing greats up close in the park's Hall of Champions.

Man o' War was born at Nursery Stud, just outside Lexington on March 29, 1917. He came from an illustrious bloodline that included Hastings, Rock Sand, and Spendthrift. Big Red, as he was affectionately nicknamed, skipped the Kentucky Derby, instead running his maiden race at Belmont Park in 1919. He won by six lengths.

Thus began an incredible racing career that saw 20 wins in 21 races. His only loss was at Saratoga in 1919 to a horse appropriately called Upset.

Man o' War's final race, in 1920 at Kenilworth, Ontario, was the first race to be filmed and shown at movie theaters in its entirety. He handily defeated Sir Barton by an incredible seven lengths. *The New York Times* rated Man o' War and Babe Ruth as the year's greatest contributions to sporting history, suggesting that the horse was "the outstanding figure of the two."

Right: *Man o' War's grave is now marked by this statue at the Kentucky Horse Park. Courtesy David Ohmer*

Below: *Man o' War in full force on the track. Courtesy The Miriam and Ira D. Wallach Division of Art, Prints and Photographs: Photography Collection, The New York Public Library*

Man o' War retired to stud and died on November 4, 1947, at Lexington's Faraway Farm. He died barely a month after the death of his groom, Will Harbut. Harbut called him "The Mostest Hoss There Ever Was." He was buried in his paddock after a service that attracted 2,500 mourners and was broadcast on national radio. In 1977, his grave was moved to the Kentucky Horse Park to make it more accessible to public visitors.

His bloodline has continued to produce champions. He sired War Admiral and was the grandsire of Seabiscuit.

Man o' War is one of the few racehorses to have been buried whole. He was embalmed and placed in a coffin with his racing silks.

ROOTS OF HISTORY

What nature sanctuary is home to the oldest tree in Kentucky?

Long before white explorers ever crossed the Cumberland Gap into what is now Kentucky, the land of Fayette County was known only to the wildlife and Indigenous peoples. Some of those Indigenous people may have passed through a diverse hardwood forest. Some of those trees have lived much longer than the local hunters, Daniel Boone, European settlers, or we ever will.

Floracliff Nature Sanctuary owes its existence to Dr. Mary Wharton. In the 1950s, she purchased tracts of land along the Kentucky River intending to preserve them for future generations. In 1996, the 287-acre tract was dedicated as a State Nature Preserve, giving it perpetual protection. Another 59 acres were added in 2017.

The sanctuary is home to an impressive range of biodiversity. More than 2,200 species have been documented, including more than 275 types of beetle, 145 species of bird, 20 species of dragonfly, and 32 types of mammal.

The chinkapin oaks watch over them all.

The approximate age of the trees was uncovered in 2008. Core samples were taken of some of the trees at Floracliff, with the expectation that there may be a few aged 100 or perhaps 200 years. Instead, ecologists found a series of chinkapin oaks predating Daniel Boone. Three of them dated to before 1630. The oldest, nicknamed Woody C. Guthtree, dates to 1611 but

---

The Trails End Lodge was built in 1917 as part of Camp Trails End. Launched in 1913 by Mary Dewitt Snyder, the camp was one of the first organized camps for girls in the south.

likely sprouted years earlier. It is the oldest documented and cross-dated tree in the state, and the second-oldest documented chinkapin oak anywhere in the world.

The discovery of these old trees has made Floracliff a place of even greater ecological significance than was previously thought. Researchers hope the trees can provide further insight into the environmental history of the region.

FLORACLIFF NATURE SANCTUARY

WHAT: Nonprofit nature sanctuary

WHERE: Elk Lick Falls Rd.

COST: Public and private group tours and programs range from free to fee depending on the program offered.

PRO TIP: Floracliff is not open for self-guided hikes. Register online for a group hike or to inquire about a private tour.

Left: *This magnificent chinkapin oak dates to at least 1611. Courtesy Floracliff Nature Sanctuary*

Below: *The lodge was originally used as a girls' camp. Courtesy Floracliff Nature Sanctuary*

SINS OF THE PAST

What's the dark history behind this downtown space?

Lexington has a less-than-admirable side to its history. Throughout the 1840s and 1850s it was a regional center for the trading of enslaved Africans, second only to New Orleans. By the outbreak of the Civil War, one in four Lexington residents were enslaved.

The marketplace was the area next to the old courthouse. It was known as Cheapside, after the historic market in London, England. A giant auction block stood in the center of the space. That was where men, women, and children were sold to buyers from across the East and the South. In one corner, a whipping post was used to dole out punishment for any number of "crimes," including being caught outdoors after 7 p.m. if you were a slave.

HENRY A. TANDY CENTENNIAL PARK

WHAT: Gathering spot formerly known as Cheapside, site of a notorious slave market

WHERE: Next to the old courthouse, between Upper and Mill, at 251 W Main St.

COST: Free

PRO TIP: Visit Thursday Night Live during the summer months at Tandy Park for food, drink, and live music.

After the Civil War, Cheapside became a site for markets and court-day gatherings. The latter were abolished in 1921 for being too rowdy.

In time, the area was repaved, and it became what it still is today: the site of the weekly farmers market as well as numerous bars and restaurants.

Yet one thing remained. The name Cheapside, although adopted by the marketplace long before it became a notorious slave-trading spot, served as a reminder of the terrible deeds

Above: *A view of Cheapside Public Square, roughly 1920. Courtesy Library of Congress*

Right: *The site has been renamed in honor of Henry A. Tandy, seen here in this undated photograph.*

that once occurred here. In 2017, the council voted to remove the two statues of local Confederate leaders. Finally, in 2020, Cheapside was no more. It was renamed, and who better to rename it after than a freed slave who became one of the city's most successful African American residents?

Henry A. Tandy was a Lexington stonemason, responsible for many local landmarks, including the Opera House, the courthouse, and the Carnegie Center. The Henry A. Tandy Centennial Park honors his contributions to the city.

Tandy's son, Vertner Woodson, went on to found the Alpha Phi Alpha Fraternity, had a distinguished military career, and was a leading New York architect.

CURES AND COCKTAILS

What local landmark was inspired by a trip to Las Vegas?

Some people go to Vegas and come back rich. Some go and come back broke. Others go and come back with a grand idea. The latter was the case for Dr. Joseph A Bondurant.

Bondurant, a pharmacist, visited Vegas in the early 1970s when the city was still undergoing its massive postwar boom. The strip was lined with lights, and the first of the megahotels were taking shape. Vegas was known for fun times, the Rat Pack, and more than a few Mafia connections.

It was the creative architecture that inspired Bondurant. After returning to Lexington, he decided to build his new pharmacy in the shape of a mortar and pestle, the traditional tools used before medicines were mass-produced. The round building has a diameter of 32 feet and is 30 feet tall (plus an extra 10 feet for the decorative pestle).

The eye-catching pharmacy opened for business in 1974. In 2033, Bondurant retired but sold the business to Eric Brewer, who kept it going until 2011.

BONDURANT'S

WHAT: Formerly a pharmacy, now Imperial Liquor Store

WHERE: 1465 Village Dr.

COST: Free to look at

PRO TIP: Feeling peckish? Grab a bite from the taco truck in the parking lot.

This is an example of mimetic architecture, a novelty style of building that mimics its intended purpose. The style was especially popular during the early to mid-20th century.

Above: *The original pharmacy. Courtesy John Margolies Roadside America photograph archive (1972–2008), Library of Congress*

Left: *The current cocktail design. Courtesy Nic Brown*

After its closure, there were fears about the future of the distinctive building. Would it be demolished?

As luck would have it (some might say the lucky Vegas touch), the new buyers shared Bondurant's creative eye. After a quick touch of paint, the mortar became a cocktail glass (more or less). The pestle is the cherry atop the cocktail. If that hasn't provided enough clues . . . it is now a drive-through liquor store.

GINKGO GOLD

What street is lined with gold?

Fall is a beautiful time to visit Kentucky as the leaves change to a rich array of golds, oranges, and reds. Although there are lots of picturesque sightseeing spots, one Lexington street in particular draws the crowds. Armed with cameras and phones, each person is on a quest for that ideal Instagrammable shot.

Catalpa Road is paved with gold.

Literally.

Ginkgo trees line both sides of the street, and in November, their leaves take on a brilliant yellow hue. As they drop and cover the ground with a thick carpet, the rush for the perfect picture begins.

Ginkgo trees are one of the oldest living tree species in the world. They grow in the wild in parts of China and Japan. The trees are tolerant to pollution and provide good shade, making them a popular choice in cities across the US.

Their visual appeal doesn't hurt their popularity either. The distinctive fan-shaped leaves are beautiful any time of year, but especially in the fall.

GINKGO GOLD

WHAT: A spectacular carpet of gold when the leaves change color

WHERE: Catalpa Rd., just across from Ashland, the Henry Clay Estate

COST: Free

PRO TIP: When the leaves are at their peak, the foot and car traffic can become quite heavy as everyone seeks that perfect shot. Weekdays are a quieter time to visit.

In the spring, another spot close to downtown proves equally popular when the cherry trees in Lexington Cemetery bloom.

Catalpa Road is carpeted with gold in the late fall. Courtesy Diana Martin

There is a downside, however. The females of the species produce a fruit that carries a rather . . . shall we say, nauseating aroma. Luckily, most of the trees on Catalpa are the male "Autumn Gold" variety, which does not produce a smell.

While you're here, take time to head across the street to the Ashland estate. Planted by the Clay family, the ginkgo trees there are now more than 150 years old.

CROSS THE RIVER

What is the oldest continually operating business in Kentucky?

In 1780, the Commonwealth of Kentucky did not even exist. The land where Lexington lies was part of Virginia. Indeed, the city of Lexington would not be established for another couple of years. All the same, those who were moving in to settle the area sensed its potential.

One of those men was Captain John Craig. In 1780, Craig claimed a large tract of land along the Kentucky River as a reward for his military service. Early settlers were laying down roots at nearby Boonesborough and along the river at Valley View but needed a way to transport goods via water. Given the rugged nature of the land, Craig proposed a ferry as a way of getting people and goods across the river. In 1785, the Virginia Assembly agreed to his proposal and approved the Valley View Ferry service.

The crossing takes just three minutes.

More than 200 years later, traveling through Kentucky is much easier, and many of the old river ferries have long since been replaced by bridges. Journeys that would once have taken several days by cart now take a mere 30 minutes by car. However, the Valley View Ferry continues to carry cars and commuters across the river. More than 80,000 people (an average of 53,000 vehicles) cross the Kentucky River each year via the ferry. Given the depth of the river here (just 11–12 feet), the ferry uses a guide cable rather than a rudder.

The Valley View Ferry remained under private ownership until 1991, when local government took over the reins. The ferry operates seven days a week, free of charge, thanks to funding from the Kentucky Transportation Cabinet and the three counties.

The trip across takes just three minutes and up to three cars are allowed per crossing. It's a fun way to experience a little local history.

VALLEY VIEW FERRY

WHAT: Kentucky's oldest continually operating business

WHERE: Tates Creek Rd. (KY-169) at the Fayette, Madison, and Jessamine County line

COST: Free

PRO TIP: Check local news for any cancellations due to bad weather.

At its peak, the riverside community of Valley View had a population of 500. Just a few houses and a church remain.

UFO LANDING

Where might an alien stop off for a soda?

Some call it pop. Some call it soda. Some combine the two and call it sodey-pop. Here in Kentucky, some still call every fizzy drink a Coke.

IS IT A SPACESHIP OR AN OFFICE BUILDING?

WHAT: Coca-Cola Plant

WHERE: 2275 Leestown Rd.

COST: Free

PRO TIP: Watch for heavy traffic on Leestown Rd.

The latter name no doubt pleases the people at the Coca-Cola plant on Leestown Road. Since the 1960s, the plant has operated a production line and later a bottling plant. The ill-fated New Coke was bottled there from the 1980s, perhaps even until it was officially discontinued in 2002.

Coca-Cola's history in Lexington goes back to 1904, when Charles Mitchell opened the Coca-Cola Bottling Works on West Water Street. In 1927,

Some locals claim the building appeared in a movie as a UFO, although no one can confirm this.

a new bottling plant opened on Short Street, and then in the 1960s operations moved to the current Leestown Road campus.

But what does this have to do with aliens and UFOs?

In a word: architecture.

The building's design reflects the 1960s obsession with the space age. Next to the warehouse, atop the main administration building, stands a round UFO-type structure, topped with a bright-blue roof and surrounded by reflective windows. To the people of Lexington, it's affectionately called the UFO.

It's not the city's only connection to alien lifeforms.

In 2023, Lexington launched the world's first interstellar tourism campaign. An infrared message was beamed to the skies, welcoming alien visitors to the Bluegrass. It will take another 38 years for the message to reach its destination—the TRAPPIST-1 solar system. Let's hope an ice-cold soda pop is waiting for them when they arrive.

This isn't the only UFO-inspired building in Lexington. A private residence built on Mt. Tabor Road in 1986 stands out from its neighbors with its space-age design.

KNOWHUTIMEAN?

Where is the final resting place of Ernest P. Worrell?

Anyone who grew up in the United States in the 1980s probably knew Ernest P. Worrell. The lovable character in the denim vest and baseball cap was an eternal optimist, not to mention the apparent bane of his neighbor Vern's existence.

ERNEST P. WORRELL LIES HERE

WHAT: The grave of actor/comedian Jim Varney

WHERE: Lexington Cemetery at 833 W Main St.

COST: Free

PRO TIP: The cemetery is open daily from 8 to 5. Varney's grave is in section C-1.

From his early days in television commercials, Ernest went on to host an Emmy-winning Saturday morning comedy show. That was followed by a starring role in nine eponymous movies. In every one, Ernest's good nature somehow saved the day. Kids grew up repeating his catchphrase, "KnowhutImean?"

The creative mind behind the beloved character was actor Jim Varney. Born in Lexington in 1949, James Albert Varney Jr. showed a love of theater from an early age. He would mimic characters he saw in cartoons and amazed his family with his photographic memory. As a student at Lexington's Lafayette High School, he won several state drama competitions.

While in high school, he also began acting and making comic appearances in local productions. By 1976, Varney was a regular on *Johnny Cash and Friends*.

Varney also appeared in the *Toy Story* movies as the voice of Slinky Dog and played Prince Carlos in the TV series *Rosanne*.

Varney rests in the Lexington cemetery next to his parents. Courtesy Nic Brown

Then along came Ernest.

The Ernest character made his first appearance in a 1980 television commercial for a Kentucky amusement park. This led to a successful career in commercials. Well-known for his milk commercials, Ernest also advertised gas utilities, car dealerships, and many other products. Since commercials were regional at the time, people from different parts of the country would associate him with different products.

By 1987, Ernest P. Worrell had gone mainstream with the movie *Ernest Goes to Camp*. At the same time, he hosted a children's show, *Hey Vern, It's Ernest*, for which Varney won an Emmy in 1988.

Varney's career was cut short when he died at his Tennessee home at the age of 50. He is buried in Lexington Cemetery next to his parents.

REVIVING A LOST CRAFT

Who built these historic fences?

A typical picture of horse farms in Kentucky shows the famous white wooden fences. While some remain, others have long been painted black as a cost-saving measure. But a drive around the roads leading in and out of Lexington reveals a different type of patchwork.

STONE WALLS

WHAT: Dry-laid walls originally built by Irish and Scottish masons

WHERE: They can be seen all around Lexington, especially on Paris Pike, Newtown Pike, Old Frankfort Pike, and Tates Creek Rd.

COST: Free

PRO TIP: Look carefully to make sure you are seeing proper mortarless walls.

Limestone walls made without any use of mortar resemble those found in the Yorkshire countryside of northern England and elsewhere in the UK and Ireland. There's a reason for that.

Dry stone walls (also known as stone fences or dry-laid stone walls) are made by careful placement of rock (in Kentucky's case, limestone). Instead of mortar, the rocks are held together by gravity and friction, forming a solid boundary. The lack of mortar allows water to pass through the cracks and evaporate. A well-built wall can last 100 years or more.

Most of the dry-laid walls around Lexington date back to the 19th century and were built between the 1820s and the 1880s by stonemasons who brought the skill with them when they immigrated to the region from Ireland and Scotland.

These Irish and Scottish masons are thought to have later passed some of their skills along to former slaves after emancipation.

Driving along Paris Pike, one sees many examples of traditional stone walls.

Sadly, by the late 20th century many of the walls had fallen victim to time and the elements. However, there were few stonemasons with the skill to repair them.

In 1996, the Dry Stone Conservancy was created to train a new generation of masons and to preserve this part of history, not just in Kentucky but throughout the US. The Conservancy, based in Lexington, operates workshops to pass on these skills before they become lost forever.

In 2020, the Conservancy carried out a major restoration project of the stone wall along Paris Pike—one of the most expensive of its kind.

A LATE ONE

What's the story behind the local soda?

The town of Winchester is just across the Clark County line, a short drive from Lexington. Welcome to the home of Ale-8-One, Kentucky's beloved soda.

We may think of carbonated beverages as a relatively recent invention, but they first made an appearance in the 18th century, when manufacturers such as Schweppes sold fizzy waters. In 1886, a Georgia pharmacist invented Coca-Cola and the carbonated drink market exploded. Within a few years, everyone was trying to create a new cola to compete.

G. L. Wainscott of Winchester was no different. In 1902, he opened a bottling plant. When he obtained a carbonation machine, he was keen to find something new for the market. He launched Roxa Kola, named for his wife, in 1906. By then the market was saturated with cola drinks. Although Roxa Kola stayed in production until 1968, Wainscott knew he needed a new flavor if he was to stay in business.

Inspired by several fiery ginger sodas he had tried in Europe, Wainscott came up with a more subtle ginger citrus mix.

Any marketing guru will tell you that branding matters, so a naming contest for the new drink was held at the 1926 county fair. The winning name? Ale-8-One, a pun on the phrase "A Late One."

The name (and the drink) took off, and locals have been grabbing a late one ever since. The Ale-8-One company is still

---

Wainscott found himself in a lawsuit against Coca-Cola, who claimed smaller cola manufacturers were stealing their name. Wainscott won the lawsuit and a federal appeal.

a family business, now led by Wainscott's great-great-nephew, and the soda is more popular than ever.

In 2003, a diet version was introduced, followed by a caffeine-free version in 2011. More recently, cherry and orange cream varieties have been added, as well as various limited edition releases. It is available in stores and restaurants throughout Kentucky, so give it a try.

ALE-8-ONE

WHAT: Central Kentucky's soda

WHERE: 25 Carol Rd., Winchester

COST: Free factory tours are available Tuesday and Thursday mornings.

PRO TIP: Try another local specialty—beer cheese.

Left: *The Ale-8-One company started as a bottling company before making its own soda. Courtesy Ale-8-One® Bottling Company*

Right: *Ale-8-One is a refreshing local favorite and is now available in multiple flavors. Courtesy Ale-8-One® Bottling Company*

PHANTOMS' WATCH

Who still keeps watch over this historic fire station?

There are those who can't wait for their workday to end. There are those who never want to leave. And then there are those who love their job so much, they stick around even after death.

Take, for instance, Henry McDonald. The dedicated firefighter loved his job so much that he was still working at the age of 69. On the evening of Christmas Day 1945, he climbed into his bunk at the Vogt Reel House on Jefferson Street and slowly drifted off to sleep, never to wake again.

Henry's grave is in Winchester, just outside Fayette County, but many believe that his spirit still lingers in the fire station that he devoted his life to. Shortly after his death, the other firefighters started to notice little things—the sound of heavy boots on the old iron staircase, a sudden rush of cold air passing by, the sound

VOGT REEL HOUSE AND HENRY MCDONALD

WHAT: Lexington's oldest active fire station and its resident spirit

WHERE: 246 Jefferson St.

COST: Free to view from outside. Ghost tours sometimes stop by during the Halloween season.

PRO TIP: Another fire station of note is The Cave at 3700 Man o' War Blvd.

The crew at Vogt have adopted the phantom as their mascot in honor of the resident ghost.

The original iron staircase is a space saver in this small fire station.

of Henry's old chair rocking to and fro up in the attic.

Over the years, the firefighters at Vogt have grown accustomed to Henry's ghost. They even adopted the nickname "The Phantoms" and have a ghostly logo painted on their firetrucks.

Henry's presence only adds to the atmosphere at Lexington's oldest active fire station. The station opened in 1904 and was named for Henry Vogt, the former chair of the City Council's Fire Committee. Vogt lived nearby and wanted to be sure his neighborhood was protected.

The station still retains much of its original appearance, complete with a striking neo-Jacobean exterior, a fire pole, and an antique metal spiral staircase. The most notable change is that firetrucks now park where horses were once stabled. And you might have an encounter with Firefighter McDonald.

Henry Vogt donated the land on which the fire station stands to the city, with one condition. They could retain ownership of the land as long as an operating station stands there.

DRINK UP

Where can you see a water tower shaped like a Dixie Cup?

A spaceship-shaped office. A giant cocktail. Lexington enjoys its odd architecture. Not far from the Coca-Cola spaceship is another landmark that deserves a closer look: a water tower in the shape of a giant Dixie Cup. If not the largest in the world, it's certainly one of the largest.

The humble paper cup is one of those things we take for granted now, but back in 1907 it was a new invention. Boston inventor Lawrence Luellen designed it as a way to help prevent the spread of germs. A few years later, he and his partner moved to New York and began manufacturing Health Kups. The problem was that by that time, other paper cup makers had moved in, and Health Kups were getting ignored. They needed a new name. Thus in 1916, the Dixie Cup was born.

The Dixie Cup grew in popularity over the next couple of decades, especially with the rising popularity of fast food restaurants. In 1958, the Dixie Cup Corporation opened a plant in Lexington and decided to mark its location with a giant water tower painted to look like their namesake product.

The future of the giant cup was under threat in 2001. Georgia-Pacific bought the Dixie Cup Corporation, and for a while it looked as though they might remove the local landmark. However, a reprieve came when the local airport said that pilots use it as a key indicator as they make their approach for landing.

Georgia-Pacific has a second plant in Kentucky. The Bowling Green location makes 25 percent of the company's paper plates and bowls.

Why yes, that is a giant cup!

GEORGIA-PACIFIC CORPORATION

WHAT: A water tower shaped and painted like a Dixie Cup

WHERE: 451 Harbison Rd.

COST: Free to look at from the road

PRO TIP: For a good view, drive to the small parking lot on Transport Ct.

SWING TIME

Where is the world's largest ceiling clock?

There is a world record holder on display in downtown Lexington, but to understand precisely how it works, you may need to brush up on your physics and math!

Let's travel back in time to Paris (France, not Kentucky) in 1851. French physicist Jean-Bernard-Léon Foucault was putting the finishing touches on a large pendulum in the city's Panthéon.

It was part of a grand experiment to show how the Earth rotates. The pendulum swings back and forth, but the pendulum's path changes to reflect the movement of the Earth and thus allows you to tell the time. A copy of Foucault's pendulum is still on display at the Panthéon. The original was moved to a museum but was damaged after the cable snapped in 2010.

Now let's flash forward from Foucault's original experiment to New Year's Eve 2001 in Lexington. The central branch of the Lexington Public Library had a new attraction to unveil. Local philanthropist Lucille Caudill Little had gifted a Foucault pendulum to hang in the library's main entry lobby.

The pendulum is 74 feet long and hangs from the ceiling, five floors up. At the top, a clock face is marked, surrounded

FOUCAULT PENDULUM

WHAT: The world's largest ceiling clock

WHERE: Lexington Public Library, Central Branch, 140 E Main St.

COST: Free

PRO TIP: The library's main gallery features a series of art and local history exhibitions.

Donor Lucille Caudill Little was kidnapped in 1979 at her father's tobacco warehouse. Incredibly, she drove to the bank to obtain the ransom, alerting the police as she did.

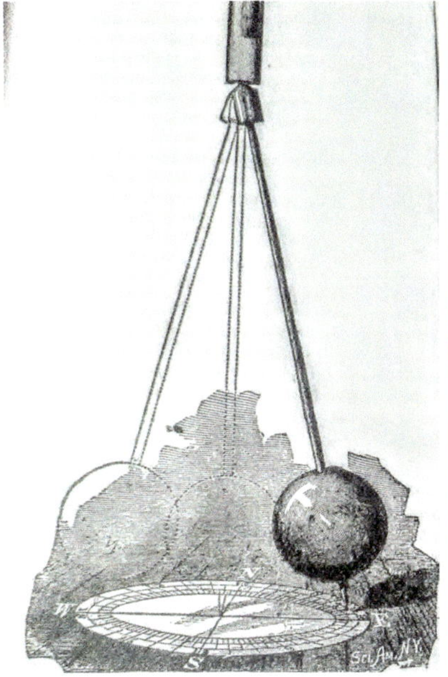

Top left: *The intricate mosaic at the base was designed by Terri Pulley.*

Bottom left: *An 1895 sketch demonstrates the Foucault Pendulum.*

Right: *The pendulum spans five stories and is 74 feet long. Courtesy Nic Brown*

by a mural of 60 racehorses, created by Kentucky artist Adalin Wichman. The mural is an homage to Eadweard Muybridge's 1872 work, thought to be the first motion picture. At the bottom is a 144-square-foot stained-glass mosaic by Terri Pulley.

Although a larger pendulum clock in Poland claimed the Guinness World Record for the world's largest in 2023, Lexington's Foucault pendulum is still listed online as the world's largest ceiling clock.

THE FINAL STRETCH

How do you bury a racehorse?

Horses hold a special place in Kentucky's history. In Lexington, the calendar revolves around spring and fall meets at Keeneland, the annual horse sales, and events at Red Mile and the Kentucky Horse Park.

After a successful career, many thoroughbreds live out their days in the picturesque paddocks of the area's horse farms or at Old Friends Farm, a retirement facility for more than 280 horses.

But what happens when a racehorse passes away?

The rare few (Man o' War, Secretariat) receive the honor of being buried whole. Most are cremated. And then some are buried in the traditional fashion—hearts, hooves, and head.

HAMBURG PLACE HORSE CEMETERY

WHAT: The final resting place for residents of a former horse farm

WHERE: Accessible from both Grey Lag Way and Sir Barton Way

COST: Free

PRO TIP: The easiest access is from the farthest side of the Walmart parking lot.

Headstones mark the resting place of Madden's most beloved horses.

The equine cemetery was moved when its original location was part of the Hamburg development.

To bury an entire horse obviously requires a large amount of space and is not practical. Thus, the tradition developed of burying the three key elements of a racehorse. The head represents a horse's intelligence and will to win. The heart is the source of a horse's courage and strength. Finally, the hooves represent speed.

More than a dozen horses are memorialized in this way at the Hamburg Place Horse Cemetery. The cemetery was relocated from nearby in 2005 when construction of the shopping mall began.

The new location features a series of grave markers in a circle around a central marker for Nancy Hanks, a standardbred harness-racing champion. To one side are three additional markers for three racing thoroughbreds. Nancy Hanks is not the only standardbred in the cemetery. Four others, as well as a polo pony, rest here.

The last monument is a bronze bust of John E. Madden, "The Wizard of Hamburg Place." He keeps a watchful eye over the creatures that were his life's work.

The Hamburg shopping area used to be a horse farm of the same name founded by John E. Madden. The streets are named after Madden's winning horses.

A GENTEEL PASTIME

Where could wealthy society ladies watch a horse race without scandal?

An afternoon at the races is a common pastime for many Kentuckians and has been for more than a century. However, there was a time when the racetrack was hardly a suitable place for a young lady to be seen. Some society ladies found an alternative.

At the edge of Fayette County is Waveland, a stately Greek Revival mansion. Daniel Boone Bryan, nephew of Daniel Boone and a Revolutionary War veteran, was granted the land. There, he built a small stone house, a grist mill, and a gunpowder shop. He also planted fields of hemp. Throughout the early 19th century, the Bryan family made their fortune through extensive hemp cultivation, using enslaved labor to produce rope for the cotton industry.

After his father's death in 1845, Joseph Sr. took over the enterprise, tearing down the original house and commissioning a grand mansion. Waveland was completed in 1848.

By the time Joseph Jr. inherited Waveland, demand for hemp was declining and the new owner's interests lay elsewhere. He transformed the property from an agricultural estate into a prestigious horse farm, complete with racetrack.

At the time, horse racing was deemed unsuitable for proper ladies. The Bryan women and their guests would watch the races from the upper balconies of Waveland's main house, where they could observe the excitement while behaving in a manner expected of Victorian ladies.

Some of the land once owned by the Bryans continues to serve as farmland today. It is owned by the University of Kentucky Agricultural Department.

The main entrance of Waveland, the Greek Revival mansion that belonged to the Bryan family

The balconies on the side of the house provided a shady and discreet place for ladies to watch the races.

WAVELAND

WHAT: Historic house, former hemp plantation, and horse farm

WHERE: 225 Waveland Museum Ln.

COST: The property grounds are free to wander. Guided tours of the mansion are available for a fee.

PRO TIP: Waveland is part of the statewide Heritage Hemp Trail, which tracks the history of hemp in Kentucky and educates about current efforts to reintroduce the crop.

Unfortunately, Joseph Bryan Jr. was quite the gambler. Despite his siblings selling their own homes in an attempt to save the estate, his debts were too great. In 1894, after just seven years with Joseph Jr. at the helm, Waveland was sold.

Today, Waveland is owned by the Kentucky Department of Parks. The house offers a glimpse into antebellum Kentucky life and the dramatic rise and fall of one of the state's most prominent families.

FROM BRIDLES TO BRIDES

What's the history of this striking white barn?

Barns are not particularly unusual in Kentucky, given that this is horse country.

This is far from a regular horse barn, however. The brilliant white octagonal structure with red doors stands four stories tall. It has been on the National Register of Historic Places since 1977, and it is easily one of the most beautiful barns in the state, perhaps the country.

It is known by many names but when constructed in 1882, this eye-catching barn was known as the Floral Hall. In the 19th century, Kentucky had a number of agricultural and mechanical associations dedicated to promoting and supporting these two key industries. The Kentucky Agricultural and Mechanical Association held an annual fair (much like today's county fairs) at the Red Mile. The Floral Hall was built as an exhibition hall to house the fair's floral displays. Local architect John McMurtry drew up the plans and wanted to create something that would be a landmark from whichever direction you approached. Even today, few trees obstruct the view.

The striking white barn is now a popular event venue. Courtesy Carol M. Highsmith Archives, Library of Congress

A shot of the barn's interior complete with chandelier.
Courtesy Bayou Bluegrass Catering

ROUND BARN STABLE OF MEMORIES

WHAT: Octagonal Barn on the National Register of Historic Places

WHERE: 1200 Red Mile Rd.

COST: Free to drive by. Renting the space for an event typically costs between $1,000 and $6,000 for a four- to six-hour rental.

PRO TIP: The Stable of Memories looks great from any angle and in any season, so it makes an excellent stop for a photo.

Later, when racing at Red Mile really took off and the fairs had moved elsewhere, this was indeed used as a barn to stable horses and store their tack. No doubt, it was one of the most luxurious barns a horse might expect to visit.

By 1963, the upper dome of the barn had fallen into disrepair. Extensive renovations restored it to its former glory and, for a while, it was used as a museum. Today the Round Barn Stable of Memories is an event space and wedding venue.

The trophy collection from Brittany Farms was moved to the Stable of Memories in 2024 and is open for viewing during race meets.

REBUILDING A REVOLUTIONARY BOURBON

What historic distillery came back to life after 50 years?

How do you restore a long-abandoned distillery and bring a forgotten brand back to life?

That was the challenge facing entrepreneur Amir Peay when he decided to relaunch the James E. Pepper Distillery in Lexington.

The Pepper brand has a long history, dating back to its founder, Elijah Pepper. A Revolutionary War veteran, he came to Lexington in 1790 and opened a distillery in Woodford County. His son Oscar took over after Elijah's death and built on the brand's success. When Oscar died, his son James was only 15, too young to take over management of the business. However, his determination saw him leveraging his father's contacts in New York and gathering investors. In 1880, he built the largest distillery in the nation alongside the Town Branch.

Pepper's branding boldly proclaimed it to be the best on the market.

Henry Clay would take Old Pepper with him to Washington, DC, to grease the gears of politics. Ulysses S. Grant and Andrew Jackson were among those who enjoyed the bourbon.

Right: *This 1894 image shows the Pepper Distillery, the largest and most advanced of the era. Photos courtesy of James E. Pepper Distilling Co.*

Left: *James E. Pepper was a successful horseman as well as a distiller.*

A key part of Pepper's success was his marketing of the bourbon. He played heavily on his grandfather's Revolutionary War roots and used bold declarations that Old Pepper had no equal.

The distillery went through decades of ups and downs. Pepper lost everything in the 1890s financial crash, only to recover it all within a few years. After his death, Pepper Distillery went through several owners and was even allowed to remain open during Prohibition, albeit as a medicinal facility and warehouse.

JAMES E. PEPPER DISTILLERY

WHAT: A reopened historic bourbon distillery

WHERE: 1228 Manchester St.

COST: Tours of the distillery can be booked through its website. There is a fee.

PRO TIP: Lexington's Distillery District is a lively hub of restaurants and entertainment.

Bourbon consumption declined dramatically in the 1950s, and the distillery closed in 1967. It lay in ruins for decades until Amir Peay entered the scene.

Peay researched the brand, collected memorabilia and original recipes, and set about renovating the distillery according to 1934 blueprints. The first barrels of the relaunched product were filled in December 2017.

Thanks to Peay, James E. Pepper 1776 and Old Pepper brands are back and reaching a new generation of bourbon lovers.

TAKING A BITE OUT OF LEARNING

What's Dracula doing in Lexington?

With a name like Transylvania, it's understandable why many visitors to this Lexington university immediately think of Dracula.

TRANSYLVANIA UNIVERSITY

WHAT: The oldest university west of the Allegheny mountains

WHERE: 300 N Broadway

COST: Free to roam the campus. In 2025, the annual cost of admission, including tuition, fees, and all living expenses, is $65,232. Scholarships and funding assistance are available.

PRO TIP: Pick up a college sweatshirt at the University Bookstore, 361 N Broadway.

Although the university was established in 1780, long before Bram Stoker put pen to paper and told his acclaimed tale, Transy (as it is known locally) enjoys leaning into its spooky connections. One only has to look at their athletics department for proof—they may be the Transy Pioneers but they sport a bat logo.

When it first opened its doors, Transylvania Seminary was the 16th college to be founded in the United States and the first west of the Allegheny Mountains. The first classes were actually held in the nearby town of Danville, but in 1793 land in Lexington was offered. Six years later, Transylvania University opened at its current location. It was home to the first law and medical schools in the West.

But back to vampires and all things spooky.

The campus community celebrates the eerie connotations of its name, particularly at Halloween. In recent years, the university president has been known to wander campus dressed as Count Dracula, and students arrange a number of

Above: *Transy boasts an impressive alumnae list that includes many political leaders. Courtesy Transylvania University*
Right: *PumpkinMania is an annual Halloween event on campus, featuring 500 pumpkins. Courtesy Gwenda Bond*

seasonal events. Most notable is PumpkinMania, when students, faculty, and locals come together to carve pumpkins. The lit Jack O'Lanterns are then displayed on the steps of the Old Morrison Building for several nights leading up to Halloween. The event gets bigger each year, with 500 pumpkins on display in 2024.

PumpkinMania is part of Raf Week. Named for botany professor Constantine Rafinesque, the week culminates in four students being chosen to spend the night in his tomb on campus.

Transy's notable alumnae include Jefferson Davis, US Supreme Court Justice John Marshall Harlan, and actor Ned Beatty.

BAFFLING BURIALS

Who's really buried under the stairs of Old Morrison?

Below the steps of Old Morrison on the campus of Transylvania University lies a tomb. Atop the tomb the concrete slab's inscription reads, "Honor to whom honor is overdue."

TOMB IN OLD MORRISON

WHAT: The supposed tomb of Constantine Rafinesque

WHERE: Old Morrison is on W Third St., at the north end of Gratz Park.

COST: The tomb is off-limits to the public.

PRO TIP: There is an annual free July 3rd concert on the lawn of Old Morrison.

According to campus lore, this is the tomb of Constantine Rafinesque, one of Transy's most colorful characters.

Born in Constantinople in 1783, Rafinesque grew up in Marseilles, France. An avid learner, he taught himself all manner of languages and academic subjects, but botany became his true passion. Traveling in the US and Europe, he collected specimens to advance his studies.

In 1819, he moved to Lexington to teach botany at Transy. The flamboyant European also taught French and Italian while cataloging his extensive collection of finds. Even so, he still found time to set tongues wagging around town, especially when it came to his rumored appetite for the ladies.

Constantine Rafinesque, pictured here in about 1820, was one of the first academics to begin deciphering the Mayan language.

Who's really buried in the tomb beneath the stairs of Old Morrison?

He started spending a lot of time with the university president's wife. Was it an exchange of ideas, or was there something illicit going on? We'll never know. Suffice it to say that by 1826, he was fired. His parting words were a curse upon Transy.

When the president died of yellow fever a few years later, and Old Morrison burned down, rumors of the curse grew. In 1924, the decision was made to reinter his remains on campus.

But who is really buried in his grave? The burial grounds of Philadelphia were heavily overcrowded in the 19th century, often causing people to be buried on top of other graves. It is likely that the body below the stairs is a woman, Mary Passimore, rather than Constantine Rafinesque. She was buried in the same plot several decades after the botanist.

Even so, the curse is thought to have been appeased, and Rafinesque is a celebrated figure on campus some two centuries after he first left.

Constantine Rafinesque died in Philadelphia in 1840. Unappreciated in his lifetime, he is now widely regarded as a genius in his field.

TRACING THE LINEAGE

Where can you trace Kentucky's thoroughbred family tree?

More than 1.5 million travelers passed through Lexington's Blue Grass Airport in 2025. But as thousands make their way through the lobby to the security checkpoint each day, how many pause to admire what is beneath their feet?

The award-winning Sire Lineage mosaic is a striking tribute to the region's equine heritage. This stunning artwork chronicles the ancestral bloodlines of Kentucky's most celebrated Thoroughbreds, embodying Lexington's proud identity as the Horse Capital of the World.

The intricate mosaic contains more than 13,000 individual letters, making up the names of 980 horses. Based on a lineage chart created by Prominent Sire Lines, the names show the genealogy of champion racehorses that have made Central Kentucky the epicenter of Thoroughbred breeding. In the center are the three foundation sires—the Darley Arabian, the Godolphin Arabian, and the Byerly Turk. The mosaic then traces generations of legendary Kentucky-bred champions.

SIRE LINEAGE

WHAT: A mosaic depicting the interconnected bloodlines of 980 thoroughbreds

WHERE: The lobby of Blue Grass Airport

COST: Free

PRO TIP: Also, take time to admire the nearby sculpture depicting Lexingtonian Solomon Van Meter, inventor of the backpack parachute

---

Blue Grass Field made an appearance in the 1964 James Bond film *Goldfinger* Bond is flown to the airfield on his way to villain Auric Goldfinger's horse farm.

Above: *The Blue Grass Airport makes many nods to Lexington's equine heritage, including this statue near the departure doors.*

Right: *Courtesy Prominent Sire Lines, LLC and Stephen Giauque*

There are more than 450 horse farms in the Bluegrass Region, 150 within Fayette County. Some are world-renowned businesses—Calumet, Lane's End, and Claiborne among them. Others may be smaller, but they still make an important contribution. Sales, racing, breeding, and related industries contribute $1.6 billion to the local economy each year.

The mosaic is also reflective of another heritage. It was created and installed by Martina Brothers Company. Established in 1927, the company was founded by three brothers who emigrated with their father and uncles from northern Italy, bringing their family trade as marble and tile craftsmen to Lexington. The company is still operated by family members.

For visitors and locals, the Sire Lineage mosaic is a reminder that in Lexington, horses aren't just part of the landscape—they're the foundation of the region's cultural identity.

THE FINAL RESTING PLACE OF MADAM BELLE

What's the connection between this quiet cemetery and *Gone with the Wind*?

Across the street from the Lexington Cemetery there is another burial ground. Calvary Cemetery is Lexington's Roman Catholic burial ground. Consecrated in 1871, it cradles the remains of nearly 10,000 Lexingtonians.

Among these thousands of souls rests Mary Belle Cox, her modest grave barely noticed among the manicured lawns and stately trees. What visitors may not know is that the plot hides several other graves. And Mary Belle was better known by another name—Belle Brezing.

Born in 1860 to a single mother, Belle rose from crushing poverty to become one of the most notorious and successful madams in the country. Her journey began in hardship—seduced at 12, pregnant at 15, followed by a failed marriage and personal tragedies including the deaths of her mother and the birth of a child with disabilities.

According to her bartender John Coyne, Belle performed "five hundred good" deeds for every bad one. Some of those good deeds surround her at Calvary. Her mother, Sarah Ann Cox McMeekin, is buried beside her, with a notably larger monument. Unmarked and all but forgotten are the graves of

---

A Belle Brezing bed race was held for several years in the early 2000s until it was canceled for being in poor taste.

THE GRAVE OF BELLE BREZING

WHAT: Lexington-based madam and philanthropist

WHERE: Calvary Cemetery, 874 W Main St.

COST: Free

PRO TIP: She is buried next to her mother.

Left: *Brezing (shown here about 1880) likely inspired Margaret Mitchell's character of Belle Watling. Courtesy University of Kentucky Libraries Special Collections Research Center*

Right: *Belle is buried next to her mother at Lexington's Calvary Cemetery.*

several friends and acquaintances. They died in poverty and Belle paid for them to receive a proper burial.

Though Margaret Mitchell denied it, local lore insists that Belle's grave in Calvary contains the mortal remains of the real-life inspiration for Belle Watling from *Gone with the Wind*. The cemetery has become a point of interest for literary tourists seeking this connection between fiction and reality, drawing them to this sacred space where thousands of Lexington's Catholic faithful also slumber.

DUELING DOCTORS

Where were old scores settled?

A barroom brawl may be one way to settle an argument. More genteel men found a more elegant solution: the duel. Thus Drs. Benjamin Dudley and William Richardson found themselves squaring off in the grounds of the Abraham Buford House, which straddles the Scott–Fayette county line.

It was 1818, and the two medical professors from Transylvania University were engaged in a duel that was rather unusual even by the standards of the day. You see, Richardson had not been challenged to the duel. Instead, he had sworn to fight it on another man's behalf.

For some time, tensions had been rising between Dudley and fellow medical academic, Dr. Daniel Drake. A rivalry had developed as to who was the better doctor. Drake publicly named Dudley a "bully and a liar." He then refused to perform an autopsy with Dudley, instead enjoying a leisurely day of fishing. When he returned, however, he was quick to dispute Dudley's findings.

Dudley was furious at the attack on his professional character, and so he challenged Drake to a duel. Even though refusing such a challenge carried the risk of being branded a coward, Drake did just that.

Enter Dr. Richardson. Dudley's behavior had rankled him in the past, so he jumped at the chance to defend Drake's honor and fight the duel in his stead.

THE OLD STUMP

WHAT: Once Lexington's most popular dueling site

WHERE: The oak is on the property of the Kentucky Horse Park next to Cane Run Creek, located at 4089 Iron Works Pike.

COST: There is an admission fee to the Kentucky Horse Park.

PRO TIP: Henry Clay's dueling pistols are on display at his former home, Ashland.

Top left: *Duels were seen as a way of defending honor, although they often required crossing a county line to meet at a place where they were legal.*

Top right: *Dr. Daniel Drake refused to accept the challenge to a duel. Courtesy National Library of Medicine*

Bottom right: *Dr. Benjamin Dudley was one of the first to pioneer cleanliness during surgery.*

The two men met with pistols at the local dueling site, a burr oak that has since fallen. We don't know if they were intentionally bad shots or simply bad marksmen. Whatever the case, Richardson missed but was then shot in the groin by his opponent. The consummate physician that he was, Dudley quickly tended to the wound, saving Richardson's life.

The people of Lexington were horrified by the event, but the men would later become good friends.

To this day, part of the oath of office for all elected officials in Kentucky is to swear that they have "not fought a duel with deadly weapons."

SHOWING THE WAY

Why is there a camel downtown?

Blink and you'll miss it. But look carefully next time you are at the corner of Main and Limestone. Around you are the central branch of the Lexington Public Library, Phoenix Park, the eternal flame memorials for law enforcement . . . and what's that? Up on a tall concrete plinth is a small bronze camel.

You have just found Lexington's zero milestone.

Local sculptor and businessman William Ingram gifted a bronze camel with a Bedouin rider to the Lexington Automobile Club. US Highway 25 and US 60 had recently been routed to run through Lexington, so Ingram gifted the statue to mark the center of the city.

ZERO-MILE MARKER

WHAT: Zero milestone camel sculpture

WHERE: Phoenix Park, corner of E Main and S Limestone

COST: Free

PRO TIP: Look up to see the restored facades of many 19th-century structures.

He created the design to mimic classic Egyptian architecture and the zero milestone in Washington, DC. The statue was cast in bronze in Cincinnati and was dedicated on November 20, 1926.

The statue (and thus the zero point) has moved several times during its history. When first put on display, the camel stood outside the old Union Station on East Main Street, now

---

Ingram was the owner of Lexington Granite Company. He also created and donated the bronze Ellis Fountain (in front of the old courthouse) as a drinking fountain for the townspeople.

the site of the county clerk's office and the parking garage. After the station was demolished in 1960, the camel, in true nomadic style, relocated to the front of the old Fayette Courthouse on West Main. Finally, in the 1990s it moved once more to Phoenix Park.

So whenever your GPS gives directions to Lexington and tells you a very specific number of miles to go, it's taking you right to this little camel. Be sure to look up to see it.

Don't be fooled by its appearance in the photo. The camel is only about 22 inches tall.

THE FORGOTTEN NOVELIST

What local landmark is dedicated to youth?

The name James Lane Allen may not be known to many modern readers, but one critic in the 1890s lavished praise on him: "Hardly since Hawthorne have we had such pages as the best of these."

The best-selling novelist achieved both critical and commercial acclaim and published more than 20 books over the course of 34 years.

James Lane Allen was born into a prosperous Lexington family in 1849. His childhood home, Scarlett Gate, is where the Lexington School now stands. After graduating from Transylvania University and teaching for several years, he turned his attention to writing. His first collection of stories, *Flute and Violin and Other Kentucky Tales and Romances*, was published in 1891.

Two years later he relocated to New York, where he remained until his death in 1925. *A Kentucky Cardinal* (1894) catapulted him into the public eye, and he became established as one of the most popular authors of his day in both the US and the UK.

His earlier works focused on romantic ideals of a gentler time. Later, however, he wrote of the

FOUNTAIN OF UNCLAD YOUTH

WHAT: A sculpture dedicated to the children of Lexington

WHERE: Gratz Park, 250 W Third St.

COST: Free

PRO TIP: James Lane Allen was brought back to Kentucky for burial in the Lexington Cemetery.

Author James Lane Allen grew up and taught in Lexington before finding fame in New York.

The fountain stands in Gratz Park, a historic district of the city. Courtesy Tamanoeconomico, Creative Commons, Wikimedia

The fountain sculpture of naked children frolicking was a gift to the city. Courtesy Nic Brown

increasingly industrialized world where "ethics were replaced by greed, honor by corruption, purity by vulgarity."

In 1925, Allen passed away. According to the *New York Times*, his cause of death was insomnia. In his will, he left a sizeable chunk of his estate to the city of Lexington. The city opted to use some of the bequest to improve Gratz Park. They commissioned a fountain in his honor. Titled *Youth*, the sculpture depicts two children, naked except for fig leaves, playing with a boat.

There is also a road named in Allen's honor, as well as an elementary school. In 2016, he was inducted into the Kentucky Writers Hall of Fame.

Sculptor Joseph Pollia was better known for his war memorials. His other works include memorials to Stonewall Jackson and abolitionist John Brown.

LUCKY LINDY'S LEX

Where was Lexington's first airport?

If you fly into Lexington today you will land at Blue Grass Airport, which offers some spectacular views of horse farms and Keeneland as you make the descent. One hundred years ago, arriving by plane was much rarer . . . and a little rougher.

The first city airport in Lexington was Halley Field, in what is now the Meadowthorpe subdivision. Meadowthorpe Farm had once belonged to James E. Pepper (of distillery fame). After his death, the house was bought by Dr. Samuel Halley, owner of the Fayette Tobacco Warehouse.

The earliest recorded landing at the site was in 1921. Distinguished World War I fighter pilot and Kentucky native Jesse O. Creech used it for his Lexington Aviation Company. A small airport opened in 1927, and soon air shows, sightseeing tours, and trainee pilots flew in and out of Halley Field.

In March 1928, famed aviator Charles Lindbergh landed at Halley Field to visit a friend. Although he had hoped to keep his visit private, news leaked and several thousand people gathered to watch him take off the next morning. He commented that

HALLEY FIELD

WHAT: Lexington's first municipal airport

WHERE: Historical marker is in the median of Boiling Springs Dr. at Leestown Rd.

COST: Free

PRO TIP: Learn more about the history of flight in Kentucky at the Aviation Museum of Kentucky.

Lindbergh's "Lucky" nickname came not from his transatlantic flight in 1927 but from two parachute evacuations he survived while flying with the mail service.

Above: *Historical marker at the sign of the original airfield.*

Right: *Charles Lindbergh, shown about 1927. Courtesy Library of Congress*

the surrounding trees and telephone wires made for a difficult departure. Years later, an eyewitness recalled thinking the plane might crash when a gust of wind caught it. This may have been what drove the search for a new site.

In 1930, a new airfield was established at Cool Meadow, now better known as Fasig Tipton, and Halley Field was abandoned a few years later.

The outbreak of World War II served as the impetus for a new, larger airport, and in 1940, 523 acres of farmland on Versailles Road were earmarked. A B-25 bomber was the first plane to land there when the runway opened in 1942.

After the war, control of Blue Grass Field was handed to the city and commercial passenger flights began. They continue today.

LIGHTS, CAMERA, LEXINGTON

Where might you find a future Hollywood in the Bluegrass?

Lexington has had its share of movie magic over the years. An earlier entry mentioned *Goldfinger* (1964), but that's not the only major feature to have been shot here. Unsurprisingly, the region's horse culture has made many an appearance. Keeneland was used as a set in *Seabiscuit* (2003), *Dreamer* (2005), and *Secretariat* (2010). There are also many Hollywood stars with Lexington roots, including George Clooney, Michael Shannon, Ashley Judd, Ned Beatty, and Harry Dean Stanton.

So when a movie multiplex in town closed, and stood abandoned for several years, it seems only appropriate that it should find a new lease of life as a movie studio.

LEX Studios opened in June 2024 and is the largest film production facility in the state of Kentucky. The building boasts more than 50,000 square feet of production space, including three sound stages, offices, and sets for every need. LEX Studios also offers support and advice

Lafayette High School alum and Hollywood star Harry Dean Stanton features on a Bryan Ave. mural.

Studio owner Misdee Wrigley Miller is the great-granddaughter of William Wrigley Jr. of chewing gum and Wrigley Field fame.

The former Woodhill Movie Theater is now helping to bring new movies to the silver screen.

LEX STUDIOS

WHAT: The largest film production facility in the state, housed in a former movie theater.

WHERE: 425 Codell Dr.

COST: This is a private business facility, but you can check for the results at your local multiplex on DVD collection.

PRO TIP: The Kentucky Theatre hosts an annual Harry Dean Stanton festival with screenings to celebrate the local actor.

in helping filmmakers bring their project to fruition.

Of course, this is all in addition to the landscapes in and around Lexington that provide a perfect backdrop—from rolling horse farms to the majestic Palisades of the Kentucky River and the historic architecture of downtown Lexington.

Efforts to make Kentucky more attractive to the film industry began in 2015 when the legislature passed a bill offering a bundle of financial incentives to film and television production companies. When combined with the right facilities, the ideal location, and an impressive pool of local talent (actors, writers, and experienced film crew), could Lexington be on its way to becoming the next Hollywood?

REMEMBERING THE 49

What's the tragic story behind the birds forever taking flight?

August 27, 2006, is a date etched in the collective memory of Lexington. It marks the tragic deaths of 49 people in the Comair Flight 5191 crash.

Shortly after 6 a.m. the passenger flight prepared to take off from Lexington's Blue Grass Airport en route to Atlanta, Georgia. One of the pilots mistakenly taxied the plane onto the wrong runway, which was too short. The plane crashed, killing all 47 passengers and two members of the three-person flight crew.

Most of those who perished were Lexington residents, aged between 16 and 72. The community was stunned in the days that followed. Two memorial services were held, one at the Lexington Opera House and one at Rupp Arena.

The investigation that followed released its findings in 2007. The cause of the crash was blamed on pilot error. The captain of the plane had led the craft onto the wrong runway and both pilots had repeatedly ignored possible warning signs that they were in the wrong location. In the many ensuing lawsuits, blame was also placed upon the air traffic control tower staff.

Meanwhile, a Flight 5191 Memorial Commission was established. After some consideration, the commission chose the University of Kentucky Arboretum as the location for a memorial to the victims.

COMAIR FLIGHT 5191 MEMORIAL

WHAT: Monument to those killed in the Flight 5191 crash in 2006

WHERE: University of Kentucky Arboretum, 500 Alumni Dr.

COST: Free

PRO TIP: The University of Kentucky Arboretum covers 100 acres near downtown Lexington. There are two walking trails for public use.

Forty-nine birds represent the 49 victims of Flight 5191. Each bird contains memories from family.

In 2011, on the fifth anniversary of the tragedy, the Flight 5191 memorial was dedicated. Designed by sculptor Douwe Blumberg, it shows 49 stainless steel birds taking flight. The names of those lost are engraved around the black granite base. Within each bird is a small metal canister. Blumberg asked the loved ones of those who died to contribute a photo, note, or other memento. These beloved memories will remain a permanent part of the sculpture, a symbol that they are not forgotten.

The memorial is in the Arboretum's Remembrance Gardens.

Douwe Blumberg also created the America's Response Monument, dedicated to the US Army Special Forces, at the National September 11 Memorial and Museum in New York.

A LITERARY PIG

Why is that pig reading a book?

It was the best of swine; it was the worst of swine!

Kentucky's connection to horses is well-known. But why is there a statue of a different farm animal in one Lexington shopping center? The answer lies in Cincinnati, just across the Ohio River, some 85 miles north of Lexington.

Just as Lexington has held several horse mania fests, Cincinnati has celebrated its love of pigs. The city attracted a large number of German immigrants in the 1800s, and they brought their love of pork with them. The city became known as "Porkopolis" by mid-century because of its pork production. Goetta, a type of breakfast sausage made from pork and oats, remains a local favorite.

In 2000, Cincinnati celebrated its porcine heritage with the Big Pig Gig, featuring 425 vibrantly decorated pigs. Entrants included *Queen Porktunia*, *Phantom of the Slopera*, and a rather literary pig, sponsored by the staff of Joseph-Beth Bookseller. Named *Hamingway*, he sports a rugged navy sweater and a white beard (now somewhat faded with age).

HAMINGWAY

WHAT: A pig statue from Cincinnati's Big Pig Gig of 2000

WHERE: Gardenside Plaza on Alexandria Dr.

COST: Free

PRO TIP: Check out one of the area's many Hispanic restaurants.

Gardenside Plaza was one of Lexington's first suburban shopping centers. Built in the 1960s, it once included an ice rink. It still has many restaurants and shopping options.

Above: *In a city known for its horses,* Hamingway *is an unexpected sight. Courtesy Nic Brown*

Right: *The pig displays quite a reading collection. Courtesy Nic Brown*

Next to him is a pile of books with suitably piggy titles: *Of Mice and Ham*, *Pig on a Hot Tin Roof*, and *Hamingway*'s own *The Swine Also Rises*.

The pigs were on display for several months until they were auctioned off for charity. If you visit Cincinnati, you will still see many of them at various locations around town. But to see *Hamingway*, you need to stop by Gardenside Plaza in Lexington.

OLD SPICE

What does Lexington's oldest house have to do with mustard?

The name Nathan Burrowes may not be familiar to many Lexingtonians now, but 150 years ago you probably would have had a jar of his famous mustard on your dining table.

Burrowes had moved from Pennsylvania to the fledgling city of Lexington in 1792. He was something of an inventor and designed a machine to aid with the harvesting of hemp. Hemp had been introduced to Kentucky in 1775, and the state became the nation's leading producer of hemp until it was banned in the 20th century. Burrowes's machine was widely copied, and he failed to market it successfully.

Instead, he turned to mustard. He developed a new method of processing mustard seeds, and in 1810 he debuted his recipe, claiming that he had perfected table mustard. The condiment added flavor to foods but was also considered a medicinal product. Mustard would have been a common feature in most households.

Burrowes first set up his business as a cottage industry at his home on West High Street. He lived in one of the oldest houses in town, originally built by the Reverend Adam Rankin in 1784.

Burrowes Lexington Mustard was a resounding success—so much so that when Burrowes died in 1841, his wife and their foster son, Samuel McCullough, took over the business. It reputedly won multiple accolades both in the US and overseas.

In 1869, McCullough sold the company to Yates & Dudley. Over the next few decades, Burrowes Mustard was produced and sold by several different manufacturers before Bruner Brothers and Co. discontinued it in 1893.

As for the house, in 1971 it came under threat of proposed development and construction in the downtown area. To protect it, the house was moved to a new location on South Mill Street. It remains there as a private residence.

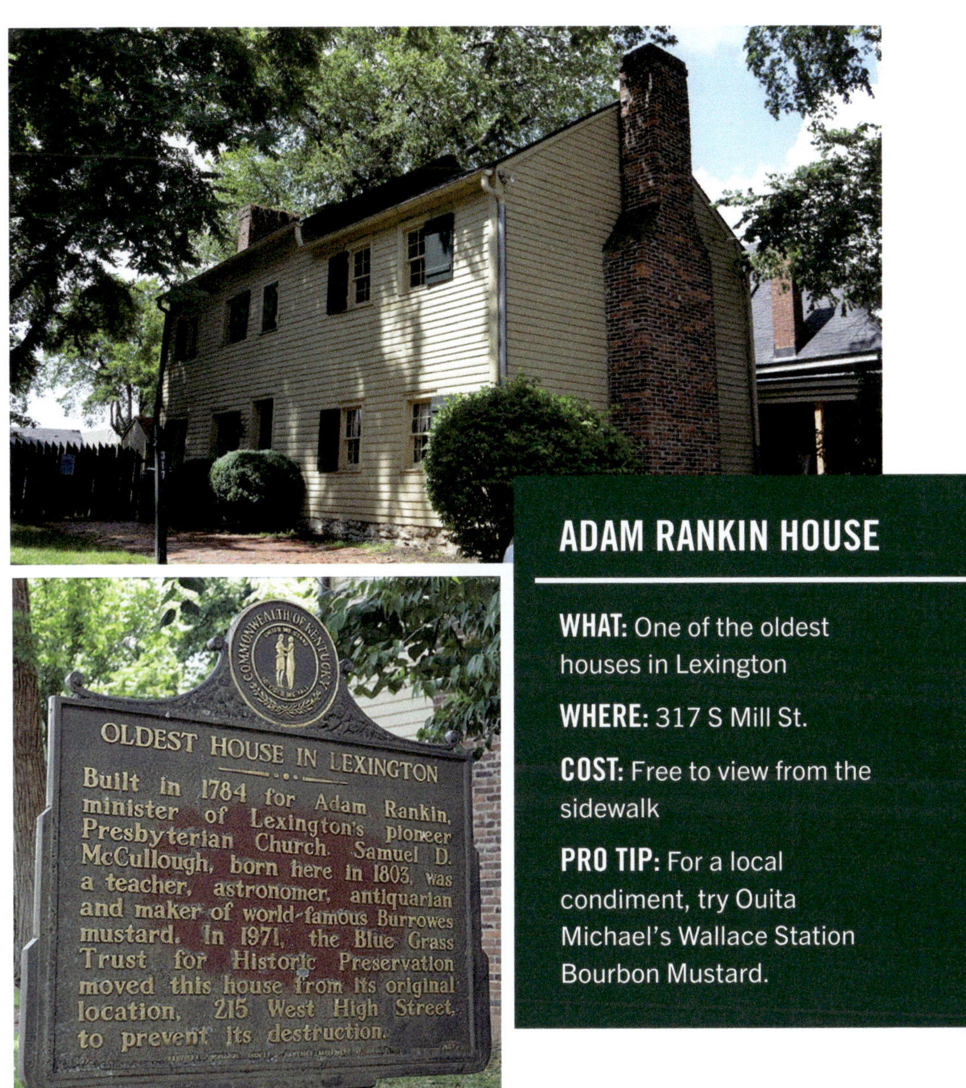

ADAM RANKIN HOUSE

WHAT: One of the oldest houses in Lexington

WHERE: 317 S Mill St.

COST: Free to view from the sidewalk

PRO TIP: For a local condiment, try Ouita Michael's Wallace Station Bourbon Mustard.

Top: *The Rankin House was owned by several notable Lexingtonians.*

Bottom: *The Rankin House was moved to a new location to protect it from urban development.*

Until the Rankin House was moved in 1971, it was the oldest house in Lexington still standing on its original site.

TIME KEEPS TICKING

Why does this clock have a pair of eyes?

As you walk down Lexington's Main Street, you will come across a large cast-iron clock standing on an iron platform near the curb. Nothing out of the ordinary, until you notice a large, very realistic pair of eyes glancing at you. Not on the face of the clock but just beneath. They're hard to miss!

This is Skuller's Clock, and it can be hard to shake the feeling that you are being watched. But why on earth does this clock have eyes?

SKULLER'S CLOCK

WHAT: Historic cast-iron clock

WHERE: 115 West Main St., near the corner of Limestone

COST: Free

PRO TIP: Skuller's Clock was fitted with an atomic clock during its restoration, so you can be sure of its accuracy.

The clock has been a Lexington fixture since 1913, when it was first placed outside Skuller's Jewelry Store on Limestone. The dual-faced clock was a way to draw attention to the business. Whenever owners Harry and Lena Skuller moved to a new storefront, the clock moved with them until they finally settled in the Main Street location in 1931.

Harry passed away in the late 1930s. His wife Lena continued the business until she died in 1984. The store closed and eventually switched hands, while the clock stayed put on Main Street. It still kept time, sort of. Strong winds had knocked it over in 1974, and repairs were made. However, by the turn of the century it was suffering from years of being

---

Skuller's Clock was removed again in 2023 after being damaged by an SUV. It was back in place, good as new, by late 2024.

Left: *Newly restored, Skuller's Clock took its place back on Main Street in 2024.*

Below: *A historic marker nearby tells the story of Skuller's Clock.*

exposed to the elements and no longer worked. In 2010, it was removed for a lengthy restoration.

But back to the eyes. Why are they there? The clock was used as a form of advertising. Henry Skuller sold jewelry and did watch repairs, but in 1913 he shared the building with an optometrist. When the clock was restored in 2013, a new set of eyes was painted to replace those long since faded away. So if you feel like someone is watching you, it's the clock!

STRANGER THAN FICTION

What's the bizarre story behind this black bear?

Many in central Kentucky are familiar with the Bluegrass Conspiracy, a real-life drama that unfolded in Lexington in the early 1980s. It had all the classic ingredients—drugs, crime, murder, and a bear.

Here's what we know for sure: In 1985, Andrew Thornton jumped from a plane while running drugs between the US and Colombia. His parachute failed and he fell to his death, landing in a residential area of Knoxville, Tennessee. Although he had a large amount of cocaine with him, some was missing.

Several months later, Georgia officials found the remains of a black bear. Testing revealed she had died of a cocaine overdose.

The stories then diverge.

According to folks at the Kentucky for Kentucky Fun Mall, the bear, still in good condition, was stuffed and put on display at a Georgia wildlife area for several years. It was later stolen, found in a pawn shop, owned by a country music star, and later found in Las Vegas. The bear was brought back to Kentucky and is now on display at the Lexington store. Dubbed Pablo Escobear, he is quite the tourist attraction and sports different seasonal outfits.

An alternative story appeared in *Vanity Fair* magazine in 2023 to coincide with the release of the *Cocaine Bear* movie. According to two retired agents with the Georgia Bureau of Investigation, they had indeed found the remains of a female black bear. Her few remaining claws were sent for DNA testing, and since she was found some three months after her death,

---

The 2023 movie *Cocaine Bear* is said to be partly inspired by real events.

there was little left. Definitely not enough for taxidermy. The magazine also reported that the owner of Kentucky for Kentucky had admitted to the story of Pablo having "heavy embellishments."

So is this the real bear? That's for you to decide.

COCAINE BEAR

WHAT: A taxidermied black bear

WHERE: Kentucky for Kentucky Fun Mall, 1315 Winchester Rd. #341

COST: Free

PRO TIP: The Fun Mall is the ideal place to get all of your Kentucky souvenirs.

Whatever the real story behind his origin, Pablo Escobear has now become a local celebrity. Courtesy Kentucky for Kentucky

A FORGOTTEN PLACE

Do witches gather at this lonely spot just a few feet from a busy thoroughfare?

Thousands of cars make their way along Nicholasville Road every day. It is one of the main commuter routes into downtown Lexington, the University of Kentucky, and the hospitals. It is also a busy shopping thoroughfare, with the Summit, Fayette Mall, and dozens of other stores lining its path.

With so much hustle and bustle, few have time to even notice a tiny plot behind an old stone wall and a metal fence. Fewer still know its history.

Sandwiched between an apartment block and a large medical center, the tiny plot stands surrounded by a grove of trees. Look closer and you will see the broken remnants of grave markers from the pioneer era.

HULL-MCGOWAN CEMETERY

WHAT: An abandoned family burial plot

WHERE: 2101 Nicholasville Rd., on Baptist Health property near Southland Dr.

COST: Free to view through the fence

PRO TIP: Southland Dr. has a host of shops and dining options to explore.

The plot is thought to have about a dozen graves (one site claims 13, while the hospital's historian has identified 10). They belong to members of the Hull and McGowan families. According to the hospital's historian, the plot was once part of a 2,000-acre property left by John Campbell, one of the founders of Louisville, to his sister's family. She had married into the McGowan family. Among those known to have been buried at the site: Jacob Hull Sr. (1783–1835), Martha McGowan Hull (1794–1845), and several infants. Other headstones have been too ravaged by time to be readable.

Vandals may also have caused some of the damage. For whatever reason, probably because of its isolated location, the

Above: *Thousands of cars speed by this tiny cemetery each day, not realizing it is there.*

Left: *Baptist Healthcare owns the property and has taken steps to protect the burial ground.*

site became known as the Witches Cemetery in the late 1990s. As a result, it became a popular place for teens to hang out. The name persists several decades later.

Baptist Health erected an iron fence to protect the cemetery. Meanwhile, they are hoping to one day find some descendants of those who lay there.

John Campbell fought in the French and Indian War and later helped to found both Pittsburgh, Pennsylvania, and Louisville, Kentucky. Campbell County is named in his honor.

ROUND AND ROUND

What park has the perfect spot for some outdoor contemplation?

"Our job in life is to find our center."

It was this philosophy that inspired Dr. Sherry Rostosky to create a walking labyrinth in Wellington Park. She had visited labyrinths across the country and became fascinated with their history in promoting meditation and relaxation.

Together with local attorney Bennett Clark, Rostosky approached the city's Division of Parks and Recreation to see if there might be a space in a public park for the project. Nearly 100 members of the local community donated money, and the labyrinth opened in 2022.

Labyrinths were first mentioned in Greek and Roman histories. Beginning in the 12th century they appeared in

The labyrinth aims to provide peace and space for meditation.

WALKING CONTEMPLATION

WHAT: An outdoor labyrinth

WHERE: Wellington Park, 565 Wellington Way

COST: Free

PRO TIP: Another labyrinth is at Hunter Presbyterian Church on 109 Rosemont Garden.

Wellington Park features Lexington's first public sculpture of a female figure.

French cathedrals. Some believe they were designed to mimic the path of a pilgrimage, and many walked them while praying. Interestingly, labyrinths have also been found in Scandinavia, the pre-Columbian Americas, Australia, and throughout Asia.

Today, labyrinths continue to provide a means of contemplation. Rostosky says, "A walking meditation helps you center yourself." The act of walking slowly and deliberately around the circuits can help a person find a sense of calm.

The labyrinth at Wellington Park provides a source of relaxation and is open to anyone who wishes to use it. An annual group event is held at the park on World Labyrinth Day, which is observed on the first Saturday in May.

Wellington Park is also home to *Katsina*, the first public statue of a woman in Lexington, unveiled in 2018.

THE SECRET GARDEN

What's the history of this oasis in a concrete jungle?

Birds chirp as they dart between redbuds and celandines, oblivious to the cars that rumble past just yards away. It's hard to visit the tiny Mathews Garden on the University of Kentucky campus and not think of the line from a Joni Mitchell song: "They paved paradise and put up a parking lot."

MATHEWS GARDEN

WHAT: A remarkable patch of biodiversity on the University of Kentucky campus

WHERE: 660 S Limestone

COST: Free

PRO TIP: Use the nearby University of Kentucky Clinic parking lot. The garden is a short walk.

Yet that's exactly what almost happened to this peaceful plot. The neighboring law school was expanding and planned to demolish the garden and its adjacent house to accommodate the construction.

The garden is named after Professor Clarence Mathews. He arrived from Massachusetts to teach at the university in 1892. During his career he served as dean of the College of Agriculture and later as head of the horticultural department. He built the house at 660 South Limestone for himself, his wife, and their four children.

Behind the house, he created a garden rich in biodiversity. To the untrained eye, it may appear overgrown, but a closer look reveals more than 300 native plants. Many of the plants

---

Clarence Mathews's daughter Ruth was an English teacher at Henry Clay High School and tended the garden until her death in 1986.

Above: *Even in winter the Mathews Garden is a welcoming oasis of tranquility.*

Left: *Buds herald the arrival of spring. Courtesy Friends of Mathews Garden*

in the garden are rare or endangered, a fact that only adds to the value of this oasis in the concrete jungle. King nut hickory, pagoda dogwood, swamp chestnut oak, and Virginia bluebells are among the many species in the 0.6-acre garden.

Today, garden clubs from around the state visit to learn about the garden's many species. Biology students use it for classes. For many others it is a place to come and find peace, a break from the noise of the outside world.

Public outcry against the planned destruction of the garden was swift. As a result, building plans were altered and Mathews Garden was given a reprieve. Still, its future remains uncertain as its caretaker recently retired and a replacement has yet to be found.

MAD OR MISUNDERSTOOD

What first lady hails from Lexington?

Her husband was shot to death before her very eyes. Three sons died in childhood. The surviving son had her committed to an institution.

Did any first lady have a more tragic or misunderstood life than Mary Todd Lincoln?

Mary Ann Todd was born in a house on Short Street, Lexington, in 1818. She was one of seven children. When she was 6, her mother died in childbirth. Two years later, her father, banker Robert S. Todd, remarried. He had nine children with his second wife.

A large family needs a large house, and in 1832 Todd bought a property on Main Street. The house, built as a tavern in 1806, was the perfect place to raise a family and entertain. Frequent guests included Senator Henry Clay, another Lexington local. Mary was fortunate to have received a good education, and she quickly developed an interest in politics. Some speculate it was a way of getting her father's attention in such a crowded household. From a young age, she was outspoken politically.

In 1839, she moved to live with her sister in Springfield, Illinois. There she met and married fellow Kentuckian Abraham Lincoln. The pair came back to visit Lexington and Mary's family. Most notably, Abe spent a month with the Todds in 1847 on his way to Washington.

After Lincoln was elected president, the family moved to

This portrait shows Mary Todd Lincoln in 1846 or 1847. Courtesy Library of Congress

Mary Todd's teenage home has a colorful and varied history. Courtesy Carol M. Highsmith Archive, Library of Congress

MARY TODD LINCOLN HOUSE

WHAT: Teen home of a first lady

WHERE: 578 W Main St.

COST: Self-guided and guided tours are available with an admission fee.

PRO TIP: Reservations are not required, but booking online can guarantee a spot on a guided tour.

Washington, DC, where Mary was frequently maligned as too extravagant in her spending. After the assassination in 1865, she faced many personal and financial struggles. Mary Todd Lincoln remains a celebrated, albeit tragic and oft-misunderstood, Kentuckian.

In 1977, Kentucky First Lady Beulah Nunn led efforts to restore and reopen the house on Main Street as a museum, the first to be dedicated to a first lady.

The Todd House on Main Street has a colorful history as an inn, the childhood home of a first lady, a grocery store, and a brothel.

EVOLUTION

What public artwork hides a mythical tale?

Each of Lexington's 40-plus murals has a story behind it, but few are as complex as the fantastic mythology behind *My Name is MO*.

Created by French street artist MTO in 2014 as part of the city's PRHBTN project, the giant mural raised quite a bit of controversy when it first appeared on the wall of an empty bourbon warehouse. The image depicts a figure in a gas mask behind bars gesturing the letters *m* and *o* with his hands. A police tape warns, "Caution. Do not feed."

Some local business owners feared that the hand signs were, in fact, gang symbols and that the artwork would be a call to violence. The nursery next to the piece eventually moved elsewhere. The piece certainly got people talking.

Yet there is more to the story that remains largely hidden and unknown. MTO did not just create the painting. He also created a mythical story behind it, a tale now hidden behind renovations and closed doors. In the abandoned rooms above the James E. Pepper Distillery and its neighboring businesses, MTO weaves a tale in spray paint.

He tells how the Volstead Act in 1919 led to Prohibition and a black market for alcohol. Then the character MO describes how he was born in Lexington. As a teenager, he snuck into the abandoned warehouses to create graffiti. Chased in by the police, he became trapped and eventually found a hidden cache of bourbon, which kept him alive. Eventually, he evolved into a strange creature, as shown contained by the bars and police tape. He concludes, "I had become a monster." MTO created

---

My Name is MO took two weeks to paint and, covering more than 20,000 square feet, it is the largest artwork MTO has created.

an online video to accompany the project.

As the district has undergone new development, much of the tale has been lost while the rest remains locked away. Few know the story behind the artwork.

MY NAME IS MO

WHAT: Mural

WHERE: Distillery District, 1200 Manchester St.

COST: Free

PRO TIP: From tacos to ice cream, cider, bourbon, and beer, there is something for everyone in the Distillery District.

Many feared the hands were making gang symbols; they are, in fact, the artist's name.

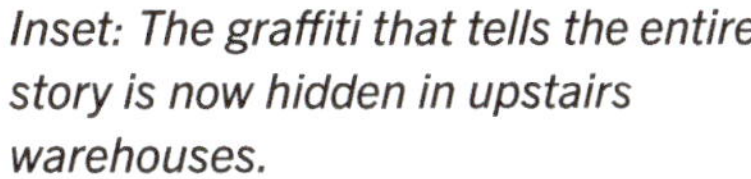

Inset: The graffiti that tells the entire story is now hidden in upstairs warehouses.

Bottom: *The completed mural shows a four-armed character with a gas mask for a face.*

SHAPING THE PAST, SHAPING THE FUTURE

Where is Fayette County's only surviving Rosenwald School?

Historical markers are reminders of the black hamlets that once dotted Fayette County. Uttingertown, Fort Springs, Bracktown, and Centerville are among them. Twenty such settlements have been identified in the Lexington area, with others possibly having once existed but are now long forgotten.

Most of Fayette County's black hamlets were formed after emancipation, although four existed before, with one dating back to 1826. Each community had its own church, school, grocery store, and more. They were self-contained, providing a safe haven from the city itself.

Today there are still remnants, if you know where to look.

One of the best known today is Cadentown, a former black hamlet near Man O' War Boulevard and Liberty Road.

CADENTOWN

WHAT: A black hamlet and the only surviving Rosenwald School in Lexington

WHERE: 705 Caden Ln.

COST: Free to view from outside

PRO TIP: The church and school are undergoing restoration and are not (yet) open to the public.

The Rosenwald Fund was established in 1917 by Julius Rosenwald, part owner of Sears, Roebuck and Co. It helped to build more than 5,000 schoolhouses for African American children.

Left: *The former one-room schoolhouse was built in 1922 and replaced another school on the site.*

Inset: *The 1901 Cadentown School class with their teacher, J. W. Durett. Courtesy Fayette County Schools Photographic Collection*

This is also the site of Cadentown School, the area's only surviving Rosenwald School.

The original Cadentown School operated from 1879 to 1922 and was built on land donated by the neighboring Cadentown Baptist Church. In 1923, the new school building, funded in part by the Rosenwald Fund, opened. It closed its doors in 1947.

Other Rosenwald Schools in Fayette County were Uttingertown, Coletown, Avon, Fort Springs, and Douglass School (not to be confused with the present-day Frederick Douglass High School).

Funding for each of the schools required that matching funds be provided by the community. The Rosenwald School in Cadentown cost $3,000 to build. Of that, $500 came from the Rosenwald Fund while the remainder was from local donations.

After its closure the school was used as a community hall for a while before being sold. Over the years it was neglected and fell into ruin. In 2005, the city council obtained the building. It was placed on the National Register of Historic Places in 2006. Plans are underway to turn it into a museum about the history of Fayette County's black hamlets.

TALES OF A TALKING TREE

What shoe shop attraction has been enchanting children for decades?

Since the 1950s, children in Lexington have been mesmerized by a special attraction when they go to buy new shoes at Howard Curry Shoes.

Welcome to the Enchanted Forest, home of the famous Talking Tree.

Howard Curry Shoes first opened its doors in 1948 at 120 North Mill Street For 10 years, the downtown store built a loyal following of customers, so much so that it was time to move and expand. The location on Southland Drive was bigger, and Howard Curry's wife, Venita, had the idea of making the space a little more decorative. She wanted to create something that would entertain the children while their parents were shopping.

Two giant built-in aquariums provided a fun diversion, but there was something else. Venita hired Dan Corman, founder of Corman Displays, to make something extra. Using driftwood, Corman created an Enchanted Forest. In the center was a very special tree. It talked to children.

The technology of the day predated motion sensors. The secret to its voice was a little simpler. A two-way radio was hidden beneath the store counter, with a speaker in the tree. After a family had bought a new pair of shoes, a sales associate would duck behind the counter and the tree would thank the children.

When the store moved again in 2009, the tree went too.

The attraction was a huge hit. Lexington resident Nic Brown fondly remembers the talking tree from his childhood. Now, he says it seems much smaller than he remembers. Instead, a new generation of children are meeting the talking tree.

TALKING TREE

WHAT: A popular attraction at a local shoe store

WHERE: Howard Curry Shoes, 2535 Nicholasville Rd.

COST: Free to browse

PRO TIP: After meeting the Talking Tree, visit the Corman Marketplace at 881 Floyd Dr. for the year-round magic of Christmas.

Above: *The tree has nostalgic value for many Lexington adults.*

Top right: *The tree finally received a name—Howie—in 2016.*

Dan Corman started Corman Displays in 1947. Now Corman & Associates, the company still creates displays for stores and attractions around the country, including several area distilleries.

WHERE CHRISTMAS SHINES BRIGHT

Where's the best Christmas light display in town?

In December, the holiday season is in full flow in Lexington. The Kentucky Horse Park holds its Southern Lights display, a drive-through extravaganza of animated lights, complete with an indoor craft market and train sets. Downtown has an ice rink in Triangle Park, alongside a giant Christmas tree and menorah. Neighborhoods glow with twinkling lights and festive inflatables.

All of the above locations are on most people's lists for a pre-Christmas drive-and-look. But out-of-towners may not know about one place that has been a local favorite for years. If you want to know more, ask anyone about the Christmas house on Chinoe Road.

In 1992, Ron Turner and his wife, Linda, built a majestic white house on the street. An electrician by trade, Turner wanted to share his skills and his religious faith the best way he knew how.

Each year, the Turners festoon the house in lights and decorations in what Turner describes as "an

CHRISTMAS HOUSE ON CHINOE

WHAT: A private residence that becomes a seasonal wonderland of lights

WHERE: 1008 Chinoe Rd.

COST: Free

PRO TIP: Be mindful of the other houses, and watch out for traffic (both pedestrians and cars).

Tens of thousands of LED lights make every Christmas season a bright one.

There's no mistaking the Christmas House.

example of joy." The display, featuring more than 50,000 LED bulbs, takes six weeks to set up, but the Turners say it is more than worth it.

An estimated 10,000 people stop by to view the lights each year, and traffic can get backed up with everyone keen to get a look.

The attraction is so popular that when the Turners put the house on the market in 2008, locals feared that what had by then become an annual tradition might end. The display moved for a couple of years to another Lexington location, but in 2012 the lights and the Turners moved back. To celebrate the reopening, they opened up the house for tours and held a special fundraiser to benefit local foster children. A Christmas party was also held for 75 local children in care.

Another popular spot is Fire Station #20 at 3001 Arrowhead Drive. The station's annual display is synced to music.

ART OF CONTENTION

Why did this mural lead to a lengthy court battle?

It is often said that art should create discussion and evoke emotion. In that case, a piece of art created during the Great Depression has fulfilled its purpose.

The Public Works of Art Project (PWAP) was a federal art program, part of Franklin D. Roosevelt's New Deal. The goal was to provide unemployed artists with paid work and to create a series of artworks that could be enjoyed by the public. The program barely lasted six months but resulted in more than 15,000 pieces of art, including murals, paintings, and sculptures.

Kentucky artist Ann Rice O'Hanlon was one of the artists employed by PWAP. She was commissioned to produce a mural in the University of Kentucky's Memorial Hall. The work was to trace Kentucky's history from 1792 through the 1920s. When completed it was the largest fresco painted by a woman in the United States.

However, history is a contentious issue, and over time O'Hanlon's work raised questions, particularly regarding its depictions of race and slavery. Concerns were raised as early as the 1970s. In 2006, its removal was suggested but rejected since the fresco was "a historical artifact." But in 2015 the university administration announced that the mural would be covered by a sheet while its future was discussed.

The sheet was removed in 2017, and a plaque was added to explain its historical context. Two years later, it was covered

---

In 2018, artists Karyn Olivier and Jay C. Lohmann painted a piece in the domed ceiling above the mural. *Witness* includes words by Frederick Douglass and portraits of key black Kentuckians.

Above: *The PWAP-era mural was intended to depict the history of Kentucky. Courtesy Marc Cornelison, University of Kentucky*

Left: *One section of the mural has caused considerable controversy. Courtesy Marc Cornelison, University of Kentucky*

again. All classes were moved from Memorial Hall, and the building was closed off.

From 2020 onward, a legal battle ensued. Activist and poet Wendell Berry sued to prevent its removal while the idea of moving it was again investigated. In 2024, the case was dismissed, but the judge ordered that the mural stay where it was. At the time of writing, Memorial Hall remains closed while the administration decides what to do.

ANN O'HANLON'S FRESCO

WHAT: A controversial mural on the University of Kentucky campus

WHERE: Memorial Hall, University of Kentucky campus

COST: The mural is not available for public viewing.

PRO TIP: Other examples of New Deal art are in the Margaret King Library on the University of Kentucky campus and the US Post Office Building on Barr St.

POOR BOY BLUES

Whatever happened to the good old drive-in burger joint?

In the early 1950s, the Belt-Line was little more than a dirt track around Lexington. Plans were afoot to create a major highway, and Joe Smiley saw the potential. Others weren't so sure. He would later tell the tale of how friends told him he was stupid to want to open a restaurant there. Smiley was undeterred.

He already owned two restaurants in West Virginia where he sold reasonably priced burgers to coal miners. So, in 1951 he decided to bring the Poor Boy to Lexington.

The Parkette Drive-In became the place to be seen for teens in the 1950s and '60s. Car culture had come into its own, and the drive-in diner was the perfect spot to hang out and show off your wheels. In addition to the Poor Boy double-decker burger, the menu included shakes, onion rings, and fried fish or chicken meal boxes.

The chicken could have gotten Joe into trouble. He named it Kentucky Fried Chicken. Meanwhile, in Utah in 1952, Colonel Harlan Sanders had just granted the first Kentucky

The Parkette's signature Poor Boy sandwich. Courtesy Parkette

PARKETTE

WHAT: American burger joint (now closed)

WHERE: 1230 E New Circle Rd.

COST: Free to look at the sign, but watch for traffic

PRO TIP: Another local burger favorite is Burgers and Shakes at 219 E New Circle Rd.

The restaurant has since gone, but the iconic sign remains. Courtesy Carol M. Highsmith Archive, Library of Congress

Fried Chicken restaurant franchise. Sanders sued Smiley for the name, and the rest is history.

When Smiley died in 2001, the Parkette was sold to several owners. A few renovations were carried out over the years, including the addition of a converted garage dining area. Nevertheless, the menu and the decor remained the same. Regular cruise-ins continued, and people came to enjoy the mix of nostalgia, burgers, and creamy shakes.

Sadly, in 2022, the Parkette closed its doors forever. A year later, the building was demolished. The sign remains as a reminder of days gone by.

In 2010, the popular Food Network Show *Diners, Drive-Ins and Dives* featured the Parkette. Host Guy Fieri enjoyed a Poor Boy and fried chicken in the diner's trademark red-vinyl booths.

FULL STEAM AHEAD

What transportation innovation was tested in Lexington?

Where would the South be without the steamboat? For much of the 19th century it was a key method of transporting goods and people up and down the Mississippi River. And its invention owes much to a Lexingtonian.

Edward West made his way to Kentucky from Virginia with several other pioneers in 1785. He settled in Lexington, and in 1788 he opened a watch and clock shop on High Street. He later added gunsmith and silversmith to his list of services.

West was also an inventor. He claimed to have created a metal ring that would cure rheumatic pains. He went on to design and patent various items, including a gun lock and a nail-cutting machine. The invention for which he is best remembered, however, is the steamboat.

In 1793, West constructed a dam along part of Town Branch and held a successful demonstration of a miniature version of his steamboat design. Crowds gathered to watch and cheer the spectacle. Decades later, historian George W. Ranck wrote, "The first successful application of steam to navigation was made." Although this can be disputed (see sidebar), West's invention was a step forward for river travel.

EDWARD WEST'S STEAMBOAT

WHAT: One of the earliest successful models of a steamboat

WHERE: The section of Town Branch where West tested his model is in the Manchester Street–McConnell Springs area. The creek can be viewed from the Distillery District.

COST: Free

PRO TIP: A model of West's steam engine is on display at the Kentucky Historical Society in Frankfort.

Above: *Crowds gathered along this part of Town Branch to watch Edward West test his steamboat design.*

Left: *Robert Fulton's* Clermont *went on to become the more successful design. Courtesy Library of Congress*

West patented his design in 1802 but was delayed by difficulties obtaining funding. Although he launched a model in 1816 that made it to New Orleans, he had been beaten by Robert Fulton's *Clermont*, which had sailed up the Hudson River in 1807. Fulton would be remembered as the pioneer of steamboat travel while West was largely forgotten. To make matters worse, West's 1793 model was destroyed when the British burned Washington, DC, in 1812, and his patent documents were lost in an 1836 fire at the patent office. No sketches or details of his design remain.

John Fitch successfully demonstrated his steamboat on the Delaware River in 1787. There is some debate as to when he patented his model.

MOBILE HOME

Why did this cabin move to Ohio and back?

For years the Rankin House was assumed to be the oldest house in Lexington. While it's the oldest house to have stayed in its original location (until 1971, that is), there is a house that was built even earlier.

It might also just be one of the first mobile homes.

Colonel Robert Patterson was among the team of settlers who helped to found Lexington in 1779. Sometime between then and the spring of 1780 he built a small cabin for his new bride, Elizabeth. At that point, the cabin was within the fort at Cane Run, near Elkhorn Creek.

Patterson later went on to help found Cincinnati. He moved to Dayton in 1803, where he and Elizabeth raised their 11 children. He died in 1827.

PATTERSON CABIN

WHAT: One of the first homes built in Lexington

WHERE: W Third St.

COST: Free

PRO TIP: Everything is as close to original as possible, with the exception of logs that rotted and needed replacement.

One of Patterson's grandchildren, John Henry, would later become a wealthy industrialist in Dayton, and in 1901, he arranged for the cabin to be relocated to his farm in Ohio. It stayed there for more than 30 years, being used as a garden tool shed.

Relocating a historic cabin, however small, is no easy undertaking. Every log and brick was painstakingly taken to Dayton, where they were pieced together according to strict

---

Robert and Elizabeth's granddaughter, Eliza Jane Brown, married Charles Anderson, governor of Ohio, for five months in 1865.

Above: *This tiny cabin has moved to Dayton, Ohio, and back again.*

Right: *Colonel Robert Patterson helped to found Lexington and was a vocal proponent of Kentucky's statehood.*

rules. John Henry Patterson insisted that everything be rebuilt exactly as it would have been in 1780.

So it's all the more impressive that the process was repeated in 1939. The cities of Dayton and Lexington as well as the local Daughters of the American Revolution chapters agreed that it should be returned to Lexington. Once again, the cabin was taken apart and rebuilt at its present location on West Third Street near Broadway. The land on which it stands once belonged to Robert Patterson. A historical marker tells the cabin's tale.

A MODERNIST MASTERPIECE

What architect created this neighborhood standout?

Few may recognize the name José Oubrerie, but the work that many architectural experts call his masterpiece stands in Lexington.

French-born Oubrerie studied architecture in Paris under modernist Le Corbusier before relocating to the US in the 1980s. He taught at several universities including the University of Kentucky (Dean of College of Design, 1987–1991) and The Ohio State University (1991–2013). After retirement, he moved back to Lexington.

Like his mentor Le Corbusier, Oubrerie was part of the modernist school of design. Their particular focus was a style called Dom-Ino, creating designs that could be easily (and cheaply) mass-produced and pieced together like dominos to create residential spaces.

The Miller House is Oubrerie's masterpiece. Completed in 1991, the 5,000-square-foot house is made of concrete, steel, and wood. It is divided into three separate living spaces that share a central common space. Elevated catwalks link open-plan spaces, while large windows provide ample natural light. The house's position atop a hill in a 30-acre estate provides plentiful views of the surrounding nature.

THE MILLER HOUSE

WHAT: Architectural masterpiece of José Oubrerie

WHERE: 832 Lochmere Pl.

COST: Free to look from outside, and if you win the lottery, you might have a chance at buying it. It sold for $801,000 in 2021.

PRO TIP: Also see Richard B. Isenhour's modernist designs at various locations around the city.

After the owner died, the house passed through several subsequent owners. By 2017 it had been badly vandalized, but a new buyer restored it. It sold again in 2021. The surrounding land has been developed into a subdivision, leaving the Miller House easy to spot among the more traditional houses.

José Oubrerie returned to Lexington after he retired and passed away in 2024. He left a strong legacy of work elsewhere in the world, including the French Cultural Center in Damascus and St Peter's Church in Firminy, France. The latter was Le Corbusier's design. When Le Corbusier died in 1965, Oubrerie saw the project to completion.

The Miller House is heavily influenced by Le Corbusier's Villa Shodhan in India. Given the difference in climate between India and Kentucky, Oubrerie added glazed windows to cope with the cold.

Oubrerie's Miller House is a network of living spaces linked by walkways and stairwells.

SPAM AND *PULP FICTION*

Where can you get Hawaiian barbecue without the flight?

Everyone remembers the conversation about the royale with cheese in Quentin Tarantino's *Pulp Fiction* (1994), but do you also remember the Big Kahuna?

The Hawaiian-themed burger joint made its first appearance in *Reservoir Dogs* (1992) and was later featured in many other Tarantino movies. It also caught the popular imagination, receiving mentions in several other movies, including *Romy and Michele's High School Reunion* (1997).

In *Pulp Fiction*, Samuel L. Jackson's character Jules describes his burger as "tasty." It looks like a regular cheeseburger, not at all like the Big Kahuna burger you can enjoy at Lexington's pair of namesake restaurants.

That's right. The city has its own real Big Kahuna Hawaiian Restaurant. Two of them, in fact.

BIG KAHUNA

WHAT: Hawaiian-style restaurant

WHERE: 904 Liberty Rd. and 3101 Clays Mill Rd.

COST: Prices range from for menu items like a Spam musubi or a coconut shrimp plate.

PRO TIP: Try the banana pudding (always a Kentucky favorite).

The restaurant was the brainchild of Harrison Ginsberg. He grew up on the West Coast and missed Hawaiian barbecue when he moved to Kentucky. He decided to open up what he describes as a "toned-down version."

What makes Hawaiian barbecue different? It has a large Asian influence with spicy and sweet elements. Pineapple, pork, fish, and Spam all make an appearance.

The first restaurant opened in 2021 on Liberty Road, and a second opened in early 2025 on Clays Mill Road. Both feature a Hawaiian-style menu of plate lunches, macaroni salad, Spam

Top left: This homage to Pulp Fiction *is among the restaurant's murals.*

Top right: Brightly painted murals are a key part of the Big Kahuna's decor.

Bottom: The Big Kahuna burger is a mouthwatering combination of beef patties, cheese, bacon, pineapple, and Hawaiian barbecue sauce.

musubi, and sticky rice. There's also a Big Kahuna burger, topped with pineapple, Swiss cheese, bacon, and Hawaiian barbecue sauce.

The restaurants offer take-out or dine-in options, as well as Hawaiian-themed apparel. While you eat your meal, you can enjoy the variety of artwork on the walls.

Jules would approve.

Spam musubi is similar to a Japanese onigiri, with Spam and rice wrapped in nori. Spam became a popular aspect of Hawaiian cuisine during the Second World War.

NORTH TO FREEDOM

What enslaved couple fled via the Underground Railroad to become Boston abolitionists?

Kentucky was the final stage of the Underground Railroad. On the opposite banks of the Ohio River, freedom beckoned. That's not to say that this final step was easy. Many enslaved people would be hunted down and caught as they made their way through the state.

Lewis Hayden and Harriet Bell were both born into slavery in Lexington. Harriet was a children's nurse while Lewis was hired out to work at the Phoenix Hotel. After they married, Lewis began to make plans to escape north. With the help of a minister who was part of the Underground Railroad, they were able to flee, eventually making their way to Canada.

The Haydens moved to Detroit, where they established a school and a church. Later, they moved to Boston so that they could be more active in the abolitionist movement. In addition to running a store, Lewis gave talks on behalf of the American Anti-Slavery Society. He and Harriet also provided shelter for fugitive slaves at their home.

In 1873, he was elected to the Massachusetts General Court, where he served one term.

Lewis died in 1889. Five years later, Harriet died. They left their estate to Harvard University to establish a scholarship for African American medical students.

The Hayden House in Boston is now a National Historic Site. A friend of the couple called the house "the temple of

---

Lewis Hayden's first wife and son were sold to Henry Clay who, in turn, sold them to a trader in the South. When he married Harriet, he was determined they would not be separated.

refuge for any hunted refugee from Southern slavery."

Meanwhile, Calvin Fairbank, the minister who helped the Haydens flee Kentucky, returned to the state. He helped 47 people escape via the Underground Railroad, was convicted twice for aiding in the escape of slaves, and spent at least 17 years in the Kentucky State Penitentiary.

LEWIS AND HARRIET HAYDEN

WHAT: Abolitionists who escaped slavery in Lexington

WHERE: The Phoenix Hotel where Lewis worked was demolished in 1987. Phoenix Park now stands on the site.

COST: If caught, those on the Underground Railroad were returned to slavery. The chance of freedom made the price worth it.

PRO TIP: St. Paul African Methodist Episcopal Church at 251 N Upper St. is Lexington's last Underground Railroad site.

Left: *Lewis Hayden escaped slavery to become a successful business owner and important figure in the abolitionist movement.*

Left: *Harriet Bell Hayden and her husband helped a number of fugitives on the Underground Railroad.*

Right: *A small room in St. Paul AME Church served as a hiding place on the Underground Railroad.*

CREATING A WATERFRONT

Where's the only public access to the Kentucky River in Fayette County?

The Kentucky River flows for almost 260 miles from its source in Lee County to Carrollton, where it joins the Ohio River. It runs along the southern edge of Fayette County through a 100-mile stretch of high cliffs known as the Kentucky Palisades.

There are views of the river from Raven Run, and you can cross it using the Valley View Ferry. However, there is no public access to the river anywhere within the county—at least not until late 2025 or 2026, when Kelley's Landing will become the first city park to offer river access.

The 30 acres of land, located roughly 17 miles from downtown Lexington and in the shadow of the I-75 bridge, were one of the first areas to be settled in what is now Fayette County.

In the 1920s the land was purchased by the Kelley family, who opened a general store. It remained in the family for three generations, with the grandson, John, opening a boat dock in the 1960s. After the dock closed in the 1980s, the buildings and land were left to decay.

John Kelley passed away in 2024, but not before selling the land to the city a few years earlier with the stipulation that it retain the family name.

KELLEY'S LANDING

WHAT: The first public park in Fayette County with direct access to the Kentucky River

WHERE: 8949 Old Richmond Rd., near Clay's Ferry Bridge

COST: Free

PRO TIP: Proud Mary BBQ, next to Kelley's Landing, is a good spot to enjoy barbecue, live music, and river views.

Visitors can explore the Kentucky River (seen here from the overlook at neighboring Raven Run) by kayak from Kelley's Landing. Courtesy Patrick Jennings

Kelley's Landing will have a series of walking trails and picnic areas with views of the Palisades. Given its location, the goal is to preserve the natural environment as much as possible, much like another nearby park, Raven Run. Of course, the main attraction will be the water. The access to the river will allow visitors to explore a 12-mile stretch of the Kentucky River bound by locks at either end.

Due to infrastructure requirements and concerns for the environment, large boats will not be able to dock at Kelley's Landing. Instead, access will be restricted to canoes and kayaks.

ROOTS AND RESISTANCE

What historic community carries a rich legacy from drag to baseball?

Several student housing blocks now stand on Prall Street, at the heart of the historically black neighborhood of Pralltown. Yet next to them is one little house that survived the redevelopment thanks to its fascinating resident.

Prall and the neighboring Colfax and Montmullin Streets were developed shortly after the Civil War. The land was floodprone and bordered the railroad tracks, but developers (all former slave owners) sold lots to former enslaved people. Like Lexington's other historically black neighborhoods, the tight-knit community developed its own distinct identity, with residents supporting each other through decades of segregation and economic challenges.

For decades, the tiny house at 186 belonged to James Herndon, an orderly at nearby Good Samaritan Hospital. Herndon was better known as Sweet Evening Breeze, a drag queen, devoted churchgoer, and pivotal figure for Lexington's queer community. The Prall Street home became a sanctuary where these two identities merged into one extraordinary life. At the height of segregation, UK athletes and the well-connected white elites of town would head to elegant parties at this unassuming residence.

Sweets used these connections to help the local community, often intervening with judges to help friends. And so it was that when developers announced they planned to raze some of

---

Other renowned former residents include blues player Tee Dee Young and LA Dodgers star Lou Johnson.

The Prall Street home of Sweet Evening Breeze survived thanks to the connections of the owner.

Sweet Evening Breeze takes tea in her parlor in 1972. Photographed by John Ashley. Courtesy Faulkner Morgan Archive

ROOTS AND RESISTANCE

WHAT: The former home of Sweet Evening Breeze and a historic black community

WHERE: 86 Prall St.

COST: #186 is now a private residence but the streets are free to wander.

PRO TIP: Visit Pralltown's Lou Johnson Park, named for another famous resident of the neighborhood.

the houses on Prall Street, she made a few quick phone calls to see that 186 did not fall victim to the bulldozer.

In recent decades, Pralltown has faced new challenges as development pressures mount. The neighborhood's proximity to the University of Kentucky makes it a targeted location for student housing. Homes that stood for generations risk being demolished to make way for apartment complexes and student-oriented businesses. This encroachment threatens the cultural heritage and community bonds that have defined Pralltown for more than a century.

HEART OF THE EAST END

What downtown venue broke the segregation barrier?

Racial segregation was very much a part of life in Lexington in the early to mid-20th century. But when the Lyric Theatre opened its doors in 1948, it was segregation-free. Gone were the separate seating and separate entrances.

This area of Lexington, just outside downtown, had a colorful history. The city's racetrack was there until 1933, and Deweese Street had served as the red-light district until 1918 or so. After the track's closure, immigrants and African Americans moved there.

LYRIC THEATRE

WHAT: Historic theater and culture center

WHERE: 300 E Third St.

COST: Admission prices vary according to the event.

PRO TIP: Tour the Historic Bluegrass offers a self-guided walking tour of the East End.

The night that Count Basie played the Lyric, the segregation barrier temporarily lifted for the music. Courtesy Lyric Theatre and Cultural Arts Center

Drag shows took place for decades at Woodland Park without police interference. Here, Lexington's first African American detective is seen leading a 1960 raid at the Lyric. Courtesy Lyric Theatre and Cultural Arts Center

The movie theater at the corner of Third and Deweese Steet (now Elm Tree Lane) quickly became a hub for the local African American community. The theater's success helped to encourage other black-owned businesses in the neighborhood.

Soon the theater was also hosting live acts, attracting such names as Ella Fitzgerald, Count Basie, and Ray Charles. Throughout the 1950s it was a center for jazz and R & B music. Community events were also held at the Lyric, including vaudeville, pageants, and drag shows featuring Sweet Evening Breeze's Creole Follies.

The move toward desegregation and the increasing number of police raids on the establishment led to a decline in business, and the Lyric closed in 1963.

After more than 50 years, the city began a campaign to restore and reopen the Lyric. Little of the original building could be retained, although the box office, the exterior marquee, and the lobby's tile floor remain as they were in its heyday.

Since reopening in 2010, the Lyric Theatre has once again reclaimed its spot as the heart of Lexington's African American community in the East End. In addition to offering live musical events and movie screenings, the Lyric is a cultural arts center and a community space. An art gallery holds regular events, paying homage to the city's diversity and history.

The Lyric Theatre's mission is "to preserve, promote, present, and celebrate diverse cultures with special emphasis on African American cultural heritage."

GREENS AND FINS

What former bakery now hosts a sustainable farming operation?

For more than a century a bakery stood on West Sixth Street near Bellaire and Jefferson. When the Rainbo Bread factory closed its doors in the 1990s, the building, known as the Bread Box, stood empty for several years.

Now, where loaves once rose, fish and greens grow in what is thought to be Kentucky's only indoor aquaponics farm. Aquaponics is a method of combining aquaculture (raising fish) and hydroponics (growing plants without soil).

FoodChain started in 2011, and its first fish were introduced in 2013. Marine shrimp have since been added to a separate aquaculture tank. The interconnected system uses 7,000 gallons of water to produce approximately 292 pounds of tilapia, 90 pounds of shrimp, and 3,200 pounds of green vegetables and herbs each year.

Water is pumped in from the city. After being dechlorinated it goes to the fish tanks, where the tilapia are raised. The fish waste is filtered to provide nutrients for the leafy greens, and the plants refilter the water that goes back into the fish tanks. The entire system is gravity-led and recirculates the water, meaning that it uses 90 percent less water than a traditional agricultural system.

Some of the tilapia, shrimp, and greens are used in the adjoining restaurant, Smithtown Seafood, with the rest

---

Eight-time James Beard Award semifinalist Ouita Michel owns several local restaurants, including Smithtown Seafood, Windy Corner Market, Wallace Station, Zim's Cafe, Honeywood, and Holly Hill Inn in Midway.

going to other local restaurants and community feeding programs. The restaurant also uses a beer batter made with beer from the on-site West Sixth Brewing brewery. Just as the fish, greens, and water circulation are all interconnected, so are the three separate businesses that inhabit this part of the Bread Box.

FoodChain works with local schools for educational programs. Meanwhile, weekly tours allow members of the public to learn more about the facility and the science behind it.

FOODCHAIN

WHAT: An aquaponics and hydroponics farm located in the former Rainbo Bread factory

WHERE: 501 W Sixth St.

COST: Tours are offered on Saturday afternoons for a small fee.

PRO TIP: Stop by Smithtown Seafood and West Sixth Brewing, both in the same building, for a bite and a drink.

Above: *Lettuce, kale, chard, and microgreens are just some of the plants grown at FoodChain.*

Left: *The Bread Box, formerly home of the Rainbo Bread factory, now houses FoodChain, Smithtown Seafood, and West Sixth Brewing.*

GOOD BOY

Who was Lexington's best friend?

We all have our routines. For Smiley Pete the day started with breakfast, usually a hamburger and some waffles, at Brandy's Kitchen on Main. Then it was a walk up to the University of Kentucky campus; Pete was a learned fellow. In the afternoon, he'd stop in at Turf Bar for a beer and grab a Hershey bar at Short & Lime Liquor. After an early supper at Carter's Supply Co., he might pay a visit to the Opera House for popcorn and a movie, or perhaps a bath at Welch's Cigar Store. Finally, he'd bed down for the night on the sidewalk between Brandy's and Welch's.

Yes, life was good for a dog like Pete.

Pete was born in 1943 but put down roots in Lexington after apparently being abandoned by his owner in 1946. The downtown locals quickly grew to love him. They nicknamed him Smiley because of his happy dog grin, but he was also referred to as the Panhandling Pooch or the Magnificent Moocher.

Pretty soon Pete was a local celebrity, regularly appearing in the local newspaper. Pete was happy to pose for the cameras in a fancy red bow every Christmas or to show off the litter of pups he fathered in 1952.

A vet visit in 1957 revealed he was not only obese but also allergic to chocolate, a diagnosis that changed his downtown eating habits. Old age, poor health, and possibly missing his

---

The Downtown Lexington Partnership gives the annual Smiley Pete Award to an individual or organization that "has a great impact on how people feel about downtown."

SMILEY PETE

WHAT: The town's favorite canine companion

WHERE: The memorial is on the sidewalk on Main Street, between Welch's Cigar Store and the courthouse.

COST: Free

PRO TIP: Smiley Pete Publications, named in his honor, produces several free local magazines including the *Southsider* and *Chevy Chaser*.

Top: *Smiley Pete poses in a red satin bow for his 1950 Christmas portrait. Courtesy University of Kentucky Libraries Special Collections Research Center*

Bottom: *Not every dog gets a memorial on Main Street, but Smiley Pete was no ordinary dog. Courtesy Nic Brown*

daily chocolate rations likely all contributed to his death. Smiley Pete passed away on July 17, 1957.

A headstone marks his grave on North Broadway. Meanwhile, local businesses contributed to a bronze plaque in his memory on Main Street near the Welch's Cigar Store. As his headstone says, he was "a friend to all."

A HOLE-Y EXPERIENCE

Where does a simple game of golf take on biblical proportions?

Everyone loves a game of mini golf. And at this family-friendly course in Lexington, you can play three different rounds, all themed around the Bible.

Fairway to Heaven Miniature Golf is part of the Lexington Ice Center and Sports Complex, which also includes two skating rinks and courts for pickleball, volleyball, and basketball.

Promising to "create a Christ-like atmosphere that is safe, clean, and fun," the center is a popular site for birthday parties, skating classes, and more.

Fairway to Heaven opened in 1988. At the time, it consisted of just one 18-hole course. Over the years it has expanded to now have three courses, each with a different biblical theme.

The first course features some of the most popular stories from the Old Testament. Navigate your way through Noah's Ark, Jonah and the Whale, and Jacob's Ladder. The Mount Sinai hole is described by journalist Alan Evans as "the hardest and highest volcano-style hole I've ever seen." Don't worry, though. The seventh hole is a day of rest and, therefore, ridiculously easy.

For the second course, follow the Star to Bethlehem and take a walk through the life of Jesus.

Finally, the third course is themed around biblical miracles. You might even see water turn into wine, but it's not for you to drink.

FAIRWAY TO HEAVEN

WHAT: A set of three mini-golf courses with a biblical theme

WHERE: 560 Eureka Springs Dr.

COST: Admission prices and hours vary according to the season, age of entrant, and number of holes played.

PRO TIP: The Lexington Ice Center also operates an ice rink in Triangle Park during the winter.

Above: *Noah's Ark is one of the features of the Old Testament course. Courtesy Lexington Ice Center and Sports Complex*

Left: *Choose just one course or play all three.*

Each course is landscaped with waterfalls and gardens, and Christian music plays throughout. Even if you are not especially religious, the three courses provide plenty of fun and entertainment for everyone.

Fairway to Heaven has been named one of the world's top-ten mini-golf attractions by *Men's Journal*, Lonely Planet, and the *Guardian*.

THE HEALING POWER OF ART

What Lexington location is the unexpected home of one of the city's best art collections?

In Lexington there is a vast collection of artwork, consisting of more than 4,000 paintings and sculptures. It is free and open to the public, and many people don't even realize it exists.

That's because the collection is not housed in a traditional museum or gallery. So where is it? In a hospital. To be more precise, it's in several hospitals on the University of Kentucky campus.

The award-winning UK Arts in HealthCare program started in 2011 and has grown in scope since then. The collection's mission is based on the idea that art can aid in the healing process. A 2012 study by the World Health Organization found that art helps "prevent illness, promote health, as well as manage and treat cancer, diabetes, trauma, abuse, acute conditions, and neurological disorders."

With that ethos in mind, the hallways, atria, and waiting rooms around the hospital complex are adorned with artwork by local, national, and international artists. From the 32-foot-tall stainless steel sculpture *Ginkgo* to a collection of paintings by hospital staff, the collection has something for everyone. Eight rotating galleries have featured exhibits ranging from photography and middle school art to

UK ARTS IN HEALTHCARE

WHAT: An extensive collection of more than 4,000 pieces of art

WHERE: Chandler Hospital, Kentucky Children's Hospital, and Kentucky Clinic, all in the vicinity of Limestone and Rose Sts.

COST: Free and open to the public. Please be mindful of patients and their family members.

PRO TIP: A brochure featuring a self-guided tour is available for download.

giant felted landscapes. The surgery waiting room has pieces by Henry Faulkner and glass artist Stephen Powell. The Children's Hospital welcomes visitors with carved folk art and paintings of Noah's Ark.

Wherever you go, you encounter colorful pieces that inspire positivity and healing.

The program has also incorporated a musical and performing arts component. Past performances have included piano concerts, caroling by the UK Opera Theatre, Chinese New Year celebrations by a local dance group, and *The Nutcracker* with dancers from the Kentucky Ballet Theatre.

> "Our mission is to create an environment of care. . . . The program recognizes the arts . . . as powerful and positive forces in the healing process."—UK Arts in HealthCare

The hospital chapel houses one of the eight rotating galleries. Courtesy UK Arts in HealthCare

TOTALLY IN LOVE

What are those lampposts doing outside Lexington's first skyscraper?

Look up as you pass the entrance of Lexington's first skyscraper, and you'll witness a tender moment frozen in time. "Totally In Love," a captivating sculpture by Dutch artist Pieke Bergman, features two working lampposts intertwined in an eternal dance of affection. Their glass lamps curve toward one another, suspended in the moment just before a kiss—a subtle urban romance that many hurried pedestrians miss entirely.

These amorous lights stand against the historic backdrop of the 1913 Fayette National Building. The building itself commands attention with its distinguished pedigree. Designed by renowned architects McKim, Mead, and White of Penn Station fame, it was once the tallest in Lexington at 15 stories. But it's the luminous lovers that add a touch of whimsy and contemporary artistry to the historic façade.

The lampposts serve both practical and artistic purposes, illuminating the entrance while symbolizing connection and intimacy in an unexpected urban setting. Their glow casts gentle shadows across the building's exterior, highlighting architectural details that have remained largely unchanged since the early 20th century.

When the building transformed into the 21C Museum Hotel in 2012, the lampposts were commissioned as part of

KISSING STREETLIGHTS AND 21C

WHAT: Art outside 21c Museum Hotel located in Lexington's first skyscraper

WHERE: 167 W Main St.

COST: Admission to the art displays in 21c is free. Fees for the hotel and Lockbox Restaurant vary.

PRO TIP: Many of the buildings on Main St. have their original historical architecture. You just have to look up to see it.

Left: *Little has changed in the outward appearance of the Fayette National Bank Building except the arrival of the penguins.*

Right: Totally in Love *combines art and functionality.*

the hotel's artistic vision. They share the spotlight with 21C's signature blue penguins.

For those who do look up, these illuminated lovers offer a moment of unexpected delight, proving that sometimes the most moving art isn't found inside museum walls but mounted on them.

One of the hotel rooms is an art installation by Chris Doyle. *Nightwatch*'s surrealist forest decor comes to life at night as lights project birds in flight and shadows moving across the walls.

CAVES OF CRYSTALS AND MUMMIES

What secrets lie beneath the city?

There's something hidden below. At least, that's the rumor. It seems everyone has tales of caves, tunnels, and strange discoveries beneath the surface of Lexington's streets.

According to Irishman Thomas Ashe, the first people to settle Lexington in the 18th century made the first strange subterranean discovery. In his 1806 accounts of his travels in the US, Ashe claimed that the men had discovered a catacomb filled with an estimated 2,500 mummies. Ashe had a reputation for being more than a little colorful in his writings. Nevertheless, the myth persists, and the claim was repeated in an 1882 history of Lexington.

A second story is that the Beaumont neighborhood is built upon a network of crystal caves. Reportedly, the entrance to the caves was blocked when the subdivision was built, but some claim that sparkling crystals emerge from the ground after heavy rains.

Further rumors discuss caves in many locations and a vast network of tunnels below downtown.

So what is the truth?

According to retired state geologist Bill Haneberg, many of the stories are word of mouth and little more. He says, "I don't know anyone who's been in the caves and seen them." Nor does he know of any published descriptions or photos.

Vulcan Materials operates two underground limestone mines in Lexington. One is on Manchester Street near the Distillery District; the other is on Old Richmond Road.

Top: *There has been a quarry near downtown Lexington since the 1890s.*

Bottom: *Mammoth Cave in western Kentucky is the world's largest cave system. Courtesy USGS Denver Library Photographic Collection*

QUARRY AND CAVES

WHAT: A plethora of geological wonders below the city

WHERE: Various locations

COST: A heavy fine if you're caught trespassing

PRO TIP: Find the perfect crystal at White Willow Emporium, 400 Old Vine St.

Likewise, he is skeptical of the mummy story, which he describes as "a frontier tall tale."

However, Haneberg notes that Kentucky stands upon large expanses of limestone and shale bedrock. The word's largest cave system is in the western part of the state (Mammoth Cave). In Lexington, Russell Cave Road is named for a cave in the area, and it's not unlikely that there could be many more. Most are kept under wraps by the Kentucky Speleological Survey for security reasons. But sorry—no mummies.

FUN DIVIDED

Where could white Lexingtonians ride a roller coaster?

Today Joyland is the name of a subdivision. Only a historical marker gives a clue to the large amusement park that once stood on the site.

Decades before Louisville had Kentucky Kingdom or Cincinnati had Kings Island, Lexington had Joyland Park. The amusement park opened in 1923 and was the go-to place for family fun and entertainment.

The 25-acre park was on Paris Pike, just north of where the intersection with I-75 is now. Admission was free, but you paid for each ride and for food, so you could spend as much or as little as you wanted.

Once inside, all sorts of attractions beckoned, no doubt ensuring that you spent more than intended. It had the first public pool in Lexington, and in the warmer months the sounds of splashing and laughter echoed through the park. There was also the Joyland Railroad, pony rides, and even a miniature zoo, complete with a bear and an alligator. But the main attractions were the two roller coasters, the smaller Kiddie Koaster and the Wildcat. For adults, there was Club Joy Dance and Casino, where Duke Ellington and other acts performed.

The park lived up to its name, providing joy for everyone. Well, not quite.

The local newspaper provided free swimming lessons for white children at the Joyland Park pool. They also provided lessons for black children at the city's Douglass Pool after it opened in 1939.

As with other venues at the time, the park was segregated and open only to whites. Black residents were allowed in the park only on a few rare special days each year. Otherwise, they were banned. Some who grew up nearby would recall playing outside the fence as they heard the laughter of white children inside.

By the early 1960s, business at the park was waning. People were more interested in going to the movies or larger amusement parks. The park closed in 1963.

JOYLAND PARK

WHAT: Amusement park open from 1923 to 1963

WHERE: Paris Pike, north of I-75

COST: Admission was free, but rides, food, and entertainment were all paid for separately.

PRO TIP: Go-karts and other rides can be found at Malibu Jack's, 2520 Nicholasville Rd.

Left: *All that remains of Joyland Park now is a historic marker. A subdivision has taken its place.*

Bottom left: *Joyland welcomed local orphans to the park several times a year. Courtesy University of Kentucky Libraries Special Collections Research Center*

Bottom right: *Boys take a swimming class at the Joyland pool in 1945. Courtesy University of Kentucky Libraries Special Collections Research Center*

RUINS AMONG THE ROOTS

RAVEN RUN

WHAT: A public park and nature sanctuary

WHERE: 3885 Raven Run Wy.

COST: Free admission daily. Raven Run opens at 8 a.m. Closing hours vary by season.

PRO TIP: No pets are allowed.

What historic remains can be found at this nature sanctuary?

Raven Run Nature Sanctuary covers 734 acres of land. Bordering the Kentucky River and providing spectacular views of the Palisades from its popular outlook spot, Raven Run is home to a vast array of nature, including more than 600 species of plants and more than 200 species of birds, not to mention deer, salamanders, and other forms of wildlife. With 10 miles of hiking trails, it is a popular destination year-round.

Revolutionary War veteran Baruch William Prather's house is now part of the Raven Run Nature Sanctuary.

There are more than 10 miles of hiking trails to explore. Courtesy Mark Marji

But while many visitors hike to the Kentucky River Overlook and back, they are missing out on some of the fascinating history that lies elsewhere in the park. In addition to the rich natural history in the sanctuary, Raven Run has several sites that date back to early settlers in the region, including a Revolutionary War veteran.

Baruch William Prather was born in Maryland in 1742. He served in the Maryland Militia during the Revolutionary War. In 1804, he and his wife, Sarah, moved to Kentucky, where they bought 166 acres of land and settled down to raise a family. The Prather House still stands in its original location in Raven Run. Baruch, Sarah, and many of their descendants are buried in the family burial ground, barely 100 yards away. Although it's now abandoned, the power lines into the house show that it was inhabited well into the 20th century.

At the far side of the park are the remains of Evans Mill. This old grist mill was built in 1833 and was powered by water from Raven Run Creek. Evans Mill ground corn for many of the farmers in the area.

Other historic points of interest at Raven Run are the grave of Archibald Moore (buried in 1871 in front of where his log cabin once stood), several miles of well-preserved stone walls, and an old lime kiln.

Raven Run has grown since it opened in 1977 with 256 acres. One of the expansions was the addition of a restored and reforested landfill in 2012.

WRAPPED IN GOLD

Is that horse made of chocolate?

Lexington bills itself as "the horse capital of the world," so you can expect to see a horse statue here and there. What you may not expect is to see so many vibrantly decorated and elaborate equine sculptures.

For example, it's a hot summer day and you've turned from Main Street onto South Upper. You look up and see a giant horse that appears to be made of chocolate. Its gold wrapping has been partly removed. Is this a competitor for the world's largest candy bar? Why doesn't it melt?

Far from being made of chocolate, *Lady Godiva's Horse* (because of Godiva, the chocolate company—get it?) is made of fiberglass and was one of the exhibits in 2010's Horse Mania.

The first Horse Mania exhibit was held in 2000. Seventy-nine fiberglass horses were decorated and displayed around the city for about four months before being auctioned off. The auction raised $750,000 for the Lexington Arts and Cultural Council. Some of those horses can still be seen at various local businesses.

The event was so popular that it was repeated. This time, 82 horses were displayed to celebrate the city's hosting of the 2010 World Equestrian Games. *Lady Godiva's Horse*, created by local artists and UK alumnae Jean Isaacs Bramlette and Audie Price, was among those exhibited. After being sold, the piece is now on display in the courtyard of The Grove, a downtown restaurant, bar, and coffee shop hub.

The Grove, home of *Lady Godiva's Horse*, is in the McAdams and Morford Building, a drugstore for more than 100 years and built in 1849.

HORSE MANIA

WHAT: Three citywide exhibitions of decorated fiberglass horses

WHERE: *Lady Godiva's Horse* can be seen at The Grove, 200 W Main St.

COST: You can see it for free from the street or get a closer look for the price of a coffee or meal in The Grove.

PRO TIP: Keep an eye open around town for other Horse Mania horses.

Top: Lady Godiva's Horse *was part of the 2010 Horse Mania public art exhibition.*

Bottom: *After being sold at auction, the artwork is now on display at The Grove.*

Horse Mania was repeated a third time in 2022. This time, in addition to the horses, which were decorated by commissioned artists, foals were decorated by local children. In all, 160 pieces went on display around town.

TIMELESS MAGIC

What downtown shop brings back magic memories?

Downtown Lexington has evolved over the decades, and many of the specialty shops that once defined its character have disappeared. Long gone are the beloved hat and shoe repair stores, now replaced by coffee shops and office space. Yet one little shop persists, if you can catch it during opening hours, that is.

THE CLOCK SHOP

WHAT: A repair store that still serves up a decent dose of magic

WHERE: 154 Short St.

COST: Free to browse

PRO TIP: Unable to visit while it's open? Check out Lexington's other downtown timepieces at the library and on Main St.

Many Lexingtonians have fond childhood memories of perusing The Clock Shop on Short Street. Affectionately known as the Magic Clock Shop, for years it carried an array of magic tricks and toys in addition to its primary purpose—repairing timepieces.

The proprietor, Edgar Hume, has been a master horologist for more than 40 years. He first learned the trade from local clockmaker Newt Nowell. Hume then opened his own business, restoring and repairing all manner of mechanical clocks and music boxes. Over the years, he has restored countless timepieces.

Sadly for some, the shop stopped selling magic tricks several years ago, and the building on Short Street has been undergoing heavy renovation since the pandemic, delaying plans to reopen. With no working phone, those seeking a clock repair are advised to visit the store's website at the moment to arrange a time for a consult.

When the store does reopen, paying it a visit requires a certain amount of magic and luck. It is open by appointment

Before the renovation, the store's window offered an intriguing treasure trove of items. Courtesy of the Magic Clock Shop

only during the week, and on Saturdays for just a couple of hours in the morning.

Those who are fortunate enough to visit The Clock Shop can catch a glimpse into a world where time is measured not in milliseconds but in the steady swing of pendulums and the precise rotation of finely machined gears—a reminder that in our rushed modern lives, some things are still worth waiting for.

Hume says the most common problems for mechanical clocks are caused by environment—heat and moisture.

REBORN FROM THE ASHES, AND REPEAT

What downtown spot oversaw much of Lexington's history?

For 180 years, the Phoenix Hotel was the cornerstone of Lexington's social and political landscape. From its beginnings as Postlethwaite's Tavern in 1797, it rose like a phoenix from the ashes after not one but two devastating fires, only to be demolished in 1977.

Captain John Postlethwaite opened his tavern on Main Street in 1797. The establishment quickly became a gathering place for travelers, politicians, and local citizens in the growing Kentucky town.

After a devastating fire in 1820, the structure was rebuilt by Postlethwaite's son-in-law. Renamed the Phoenix Hotel, it flourished as Lexington grew into a prominent city, hosting countless distinguished guests and serving as the backdrop for pivotal moments in Kentucky history, both good and bad.

In 1833, Postlethwaite and a number of guests at the Phoenix fell victim to the cholera outbreak, caused by polluted

SITE OF THE PHOENIX HOTEL

WHAT: Now a public park, once Lexington's historic tavern

WHERE: 100 E Main St.

COST: Free

PRO TIP: While at Phoenix Park, be sure to visit the camel mile marker and the pendulum clock in the neighboring library.

Among the guests to have stayed at the tavern is one Colonel Burr, the former vice president, known for his duel with Alexander Hamilton.

Above: *Revolutionary War veteran and founder of the tavern bearing his name, Captain Postlethwaite is seen here in this Jouett portrait.*

Left: *A 1919 postcard depicting the Phoenix Hotel*

water from the Town Branch which ran behind the hotel. Later, during the Civil War, both sides used it for lodging and meetings. Confederate Colonel John Hunt Morgan retreated there after the Battle of Perryville, and the Union used it as their headquarters for a while.

Disaster struck again in 1879 when flames engulfed the building, but true to its name, the Phoenix rose once more. The new rebuilt version featured modern improvements such as steam heat and running water in each room.

During the Civil Rights Movement, its policies of segregation attracted attention. The Congress of Racial Equality (CORE) organized several protests after Boston Celtics players were prevented from staying there.

Despite its historical significance, the Phoenix Hotel couldn't compete with modern hotel chains and changing downtown dynamics. It closed its doors in 1977 and was demolished in 1981, making way for what is now Phoenix Park.

A MUSEUM OF GEMS AND SHELLS

Where can you visit a grotto inspired by Versailles?

Within the elaborate grounds of the Palace of Versailles (in France, *not* the Castle down the road from Lexington), the Grotto of Thetis featured an interior decorated with shells, designed to resemble a magical sea cave. It is likely that George Headley III visited the palace as a student in Paris, and that it inspired his own shell creation at his home in Lexington.

Born in 1908 in Virginia, Headley went on to live a life of glitz, studying art in Paris and then designing jewelry for the rich and famous of Los Angeles society. By 1949 he wanted a change from life on the West Coast. He moved to Lexington. He continued to make his bejeweled creations and mingle with the rich and famous, this time Kentucky's wealthy horse set.

A jewel heist in 1994 resulted in $1.6 million of gems being stolen from the Headley-Whitney Museum. The thieves were caught five years later, but the gems were never recovered.

The Horse Mania entry was inspired by the shell grotto at Headley-Whitney.

Did the Grotto of Thetis at Versailles serve as inspiration for Headley's own shell grotto?

SHELL GROTTO AT THE HEADLEY-WHITNEY MUSEUM

WHAT: Museum displaying the collections of George Headley III and his family

WHERE: 4435 Old Frankfort Pike

COST: The museum charges an admission fee.

PRO TIP: The Headley-Whitney Museum is surrounded by farms, so a visit includes a glimpse of rural horse country.

In 1968, Headley designed a museum to show off his jewel collection to the public. At the time, he assumed that his family and friends would be the only ones interested. Instead, the museum was an instant success. It has expanded several times in its history and now houses a range of art as well as the dollhouse collection of Marylou Whitney, Headley's sister-in-law.

There's also the shell grotto. The garage was transformed in 1973. Headley spent a year decorating the room with all manner of shells, while artist Carl Malouf created a set of mosaics for the ceiling. The grotto remains one of the attractions at the Headley-Whitney Museum. It even inspired an exhibit in the 2010 Horse Mania event.

Holly Johnson, a Pensacola Beach artist, covered one of the fiberglass horses with thousands of tiny shells to create *A Horse of a Different Shell*. The artwork is on permanent display in the grounds of the Headley-Whitney.

HIDDEN BUT REVEALED

TOWN BRANCH

WHAT: The creek that Lexington grew up around

WHERE: Visible at several locations in downtown Lexington

COST: Free

PRO TIP: The park is due to open in 2025 and will include play areas, walking trails, and an open-air amphitheater.

Why was the waterway under Lexington covered and then uncovered again?

Fayette County is bordered by the Kentucky River, but another waterway flows through the heart of Lexington. It made Lexington the city it is today. So where has it been hiding all these years?

When settlers arrived in what is now Lexington, the Middle Fork of the Elkhorn, better known as Town Branch, was a vital source of fresh water. As the fledgling town grew, so did the creek's importance, providing water for bourbon distilleries and grist mills.

Even from a relatively early point in Lexington's history, there were problems with the Town Branch. As the only source of water, it was key to industry and everyday life. At the same time, it quickly became polluted as there was nowhere else for waste to go but back into the very same creek. Flooding and lack of sanitation in the water supply caused deadly cholera outbreaks in 1833 and 1849. Flooding continued through the years,

Above: *The construction of Gatton Park on the Town Branch saw the waterway revealed again for the first time in nearly 100 years.*

Opposite: *Town Branch is clearly visible in the Distillery District.*

causing ever-increasing problems. The downtown area suffered from heavy flash floods in 1928 and again in 1932.

On April 28, 1934, the James E. Pepper Distillery caught fire, after a night watchman mistakenly poured gasoline instead of kerosene into the stove. The blaze destroyed seven buildings and sent 15,000 gallons of burning whisky into the waters of the Town Branch. What alcohol didn't burn off was ingested by the creek's fish. Newspaper reports tell of fishermen and locals near Weisenberger's Mill, 12 miles away, scooping the inebriated fish into their nets. Truly the catch of the day!

A few weeks after the fire, the Town Branch was buried underground as a storm sewer. Just like that, the Town Branch was gone, buried under layers of concrete. Water and Vine Streets marked where the waters once ran. Over time, people forgot that there had even been a river running through the city, although it still flowed above ground through the Distillery District.

Parts of the creek have been uncovered to develop Gatton Park on the Town Branch. The waterfront park allows visitors to enjoy the creek once more.

A BOHEMIAN SANCTUARY

What Lexington home hosted a menagerie and welcomed Tennessee Williams as a guest?

To look at a Henry Faulkner painting is to enter a world of surreal, fantastical landscapes depicted in vivid color. His former Lexington home was equally wild and colorful.

Faulkner's home on West Third Street in Lexington was an impressive Italianate-Romanesque structure built in 1882. The architectural details of the home—with its distinctive arched windows, ornate cornices, and decorative brickwork—provided a fitting backdrop for Faulkner's artistic lifestyle.

The artist purchased the home in the 1960s and lived there periodically until his death in 1981. He converted the historic property into three separate apartments, maintaining one for himself while hosting an array of guests and friends in the others.

THE ARTIST'S HOME

WHAT: An Italianate home formerly owned by artist Henry Faulkner.

WHERE: 462 West Third St.

COST: Now a private resident but free to view from the sidewalk.

PRO TIP: Third Street is within walking distance of downtown Lexington and is also close to many restaurants and bars on Jefferson.

The house served as both living space and artistic sanctuary, filled with an eclectic collection of furnishings, artwork, and his collection of beloved animals. Most famous was his pet goat Alice, now legendary among locals for her reputed love of bourbon (although this has been disputed by some of Faulkner's associates).

Faulkner split his time between Lexington and his Key West property, but when he was in town, the house was a gathering

Above: *The former home of colorful artist Henry Faulkner is now a quiet family home.*

Left: *Henry with his beloved goat, Alice. Photographer unknown. Made available through Creative Commons license (flickr.com/photos/keyslibraries/12388868113).*

place for artists, writers, and intellectuals. Author, playwright, and close friend of Faulkner, Tennessee Williams was among the famous guests.

After Faulkner's death, the house remained empty for some time and fell into disrepair. In 2013, with new owners, the house underwent a complete restoration, returning it to its former glory as a single-family residence. And preserving the architectural heritage that once housed one of Kentucky's most colorful artistic personalities.

Pieces of Faulkner's art are usually on display in the UK Arts in HealthCare collection and at Fine Art Editions, 190 Jefferson St.

ROBOTS AND RAMEN

What business was behind the rise of a Japanese community in central Kentucky?

In 1988 the first Toyota Camry rolled off the production line in Georgetown, Kentucky. Just two years earlier, construction had begun at the factory amid great fanfare of what it would mean for the state.

At the time, Georgetown was a small town of about 11,000 people 18 miles north of Lexington. Today, it has a population of more than 40,000. Much of that growth has been a result of the automotive plant, Toyota's largest vehicle manufacturing plant in the world.

Since 1988, a sizeable Japanese community has grown in central Kentucky, mainly in Georgetown and Lexington. In addition to the many Japanese companies that have opened factories and warehouses in the area, there is a Japanese school to provide education for the children on Saturdays, Japanese food shops, and Japanese restaurants.

Despite being 600 miles from the nearest coast (Virginia Beach), Lexington has developed a love of sushi, with people driving up from Eastern Kentucky on the weekends to enjoy some hibachi and a spicy tuna roll. Even the local supermarkets now have sushi counters.

One of these restaurants, Zundo, features something extra. They offer a variety of ramen dishes, with their ramen noodles made fresh in-house. What's more, your order is delivered to you via robot! That's right, much to the delight of customers of

---

Lexington is twinned with Shinhidaka on the island of Hokkaido. Both cities share a mutual love of horses, with Shinhidaka home to the largest horse sales location in Japan.

ZUNDO

WHAT: Japanese restaurant

WHERE: 127 W Tiverton Wy. #184

COST: Toku Revolving Sushi charges per plate of sushi; appetizers typically start at $6 in Zundo

PRO TIP: Most Japanese restaurants feature some special rolls with a local twist. Look out for a Wildcat or Bluegrass roll.

Top left: *Fresh ramen noodles are made on the premises at Zundo. Courtesy Nic Brown*

Top right: *A special conveyor belt will deliver your sushi. Courtesy Nic Brown*

Above: *Be sure to thank your robot when it brings your food. Courtesy Nic Brown*

all ages, your food will arrive on a talking cat robot. It will thank you, wish you a nice meal, and even express its joy if you pet it. If you prefer to skip the robots, you can dine at the connected restaurant next door, which delivers sushi via a conveyor belt. Order a special roll and it will be delivered by mini race car.

Who said food was boring?

Itadakimasu!

MAGIC PAT-LAND

Where do art and social activism meet for a cup of coffee?

Every college town has that one special place. The place where people meet for coffee, perhaps a bite to eat. A place where they can chat with friends or work undisturbed on their laptops. A place with a little more than the usual coffee shop. A place that feels like the beating heart of a community.

THIRD STREET STUFF

WHAT: Coffee shop with a vibrant dose of art and social activism

WHERE: 257 N Limestone

COST: Coffee and sandwiches are very reasonably priced.

PRO TIP: Try an Isaac Murphy (hazelnut and praline) or a Sojourner Truth (toffee mocha).

In Lexington, that place is Third Street Stuff, or, as local chef Ouita Michel has called it, Magic Pat-land.

The Pat is question is owner Pat Gerhard. She first opened Third Street Stuff in 1996 as a funky little gift shop where you could buy Frida Kahlo socks or a whimsical bumper sticker. In 2004, she added a coffee shop. Over time, that has taken over, although you can still buy a few fun knickknacks.

Left: *Inside, settle down in a cozy corner with a book and a coffee.*

Opposite: *The decorated outside gives a hint that Third Street Stuff is no ordinary coffee shop.*

Whether it is providing coffee or trinkets, Third Street Stuff makes you feel as if you're entering wonderland. An artist by training, Pat has covered every inch of free space in color. Handmade art adorns the walls alongside newspaper clippings, vintage photos, and inspirational quotes. Outside, Black Lives Matter and Pride flags proudly support the "welcome friends" message by the door.

This isn't just a place to get coffee and enjoy the atmosphere. This is a safe space for everyone. On any given day, you might find local groups here designing a new green space or making posters for an upcoming event. And Pat is usually bustling around, making drinks, chatting to customers, or adding the latest splash of color.

This is, indeed, Magic Pat-land.

In 2014, *Business Insider* named Third Street Stuff the best coffee shop in Kentucky, praising its "colorful, funky vibe."

WHERE MENTAL HEALTH CARE BEGAN

Where was the second mental health hospital in the nation?

Mental health care in the early 19th century was in its infancy. The first public psychiatric hospital opened in Williamsburg, Virginia, in 1766. Kentuckians who needed hospitalization were sent there.

In 1816, a group of Lexington civic leaders decided to establish something closer to home. The state passed an "act to establish a lunatic asylum" in 1822 and chose the site where Fayette Hospital was under construction. The asylum opened in 1824 on a vast 400-acre lot. For the most part, it was a self-contained community. Staff lived on-site, and, with the help of the residents, they grew and raised the hospital's food.

Within a year of opening, overcrowding was a problem, and several additional wings were built over the years. Later, a separate wing was added for female patients. Patients from wealthier backgrounds received preferential treatment, including private rooms as opposed to the open wards provided for most residents.

The forms of treatment used changed enormously during the hospital's 200-year history. The earliest patients were likely left to their own devices with only the most dangerous locked in cells. Gradually, emphasis was placed on providing

EASTERN STATE HOSPITAL

WHAT: The second mental hospital in the United States

WHERE: 500 Newtown Pike, now the site of Bluegrass Community and Technical College

COST: Free to wander the campus grounds

PRO TIP: A small hospital cemetery has been left untouched on the campus.

a quiet atmosphere with plenty of fresh air and work. By the 20th century, treatment had turned to newer, often surgical methods. By the end of World War II, the population at Eastern State Hospital (the name since 1912) reached 2,000. Electroshock therapy and lobotomies were common for a time until modern pharmaceutical treatments became the norm.

By the 21st century, the buildings were in desperate need of renovation. Patients were moved to a new site in 2013 on Bull Lea Road. The original facility on Newtown Pike was demolished the next year. Bluegrass Community and Technical College now has a campus there.

In the late 19th century, annual lunatic balls were held at Eastern State and at other asylums. The social elite would attend, and it was considered a form of civic duty.

Given the name, this picture of the Eastern Kentucky Asylum for the Insane can be dated to between 1894 and 1912. Courtesy Lexington History Museum

STILL KEEPING HOUSE

Does the former mistress of this historic house still roam its halls?

The Bodley-Bullock House has seen Lexington change a great deal since it was first built in 1814. But is it possible that its last resident is the one who has chosen to stay?

The Federal-style house, named for early owner and Revolutionary War veteran General Thomas Bodley, was truly a house divided during the American Civil War. At various points throughout the war, it served as a headquarters for both the Union and Confederacy. After the war, it had several owners before becoming the home of the Bullocks in 1912.

Dr. Waller Bullock founded the Lexington Clinic and was an avid sculptor in his spare time. Some of his pieces are still on display in the house today. His wife, Minnie Pettit Bullock, was affectionately referred to as Miss Minnie. Miss Minnie was a strict teetotaler, in sharp contrast to her husband, who would frequently hide alcohol in the house. The couple had no children, and she was said to have disliked them.

Dr. Bullock passed away in 1952, but Miss Minnie remained alone at the house until her death in 1970. In her will, she bequeathed the house to Transylvania University, with the request that it become a museum. The will also stipulated that no alcohol should be served. The Junior League of Lexington now oversees the house, opening it to the public several times a year, and renting it as an event space for weddings.

Shortly after a vote was taken to approve the serving of alcohol at events, a glass tabletop cracked from end to end. Another time, a young boy, sleeping in Miss Minnie's

---

Minnie Bullock was a very keen gardener and a founding member of the Garden Club of Lexington in 1916.

GHOST OF MINNIE BULLOCK

WHAT: Last owner of the Bodley-Bullock House at the corner of Gratz Park

WHERE: 200 Market St.

COST: Free admission during specific events

PRO TIP: The Bodley-Bullock House is open to the public during the Lexington Gallery Hop, held six times a year from 5 to 8 p.m.

Top: *The Bodley-Bullock House, seen here in 1940, stands at one of the corners of Gratz Park. Courtesy Library of Congress*

Bottom: *Does Miss Minnie still keep an eye on things in her bedroom (seen here) and elsewhere in the house?*

bedroom during an event, ran downstairs saying he had been chased out by an old lady. A shadowy figure has appeared in some wedding photos.

Miss Minnie is still taking an interest.

ECHOES OF THE SILVER SCREEN

Where can you still enjoy organ music before a movie screening?

It's not very often now that you go to a movie theater to find your screening is preceded by a good dose of organ music. Then again, the Kentucky Theatre is far from your standard multiplex.

The Kentucky opened in October 1922 with a screening of *The Eternal Flame* starring Norma Talmadge and Adolphe Menjou. Moviegoers were treated to a truly sumptuous setting with marble decor, seating for 1,200 people (whites only; there was no balcony), and a Wurlitzer organ. It was immediately proclaimed one of the finest theaters in the nation and would later be one of the first to prepare for talkies with the installation of sound equipment.

The Wurlitzer organ was a huge draw. Capable of providing a rich sound like no other, it was said to have cost $25,000. It could provide a whole array of sound effects to accompany a movie, and well-known organists traveled to Lexington just to play it. Unfortunately, the downtown

---

The smaller State Theatre, next to the Kentucky, was built in 1926 and accommodated a segregated audience. It was renovated in the 1990s and is now a second screen at the Kentucky.

Above: *The Kentucky Theatre first welcomed moviegoers in 1922.*

Opposite: *The Wurlitzer console has been restored to its original glory. Courtesy Bluegrass Chapter of the American Theatre Organ Society*

floods in 1928 all but destroyed the Wurlitzer, and it lay dormant for decades, slowly rotting.

In 1977, the organ was sold. It found its way to the University of Kentucky and then to a local buyer who had hopes of restoring it. It is now in the hands of the Bluegrass Chapter of the American Theatre Organ Society (BGATOS). They plan to repair and restore the organ in full so that it can be reinstalled in the Kentucky.

Until the Wurlitzer is fully restored and replaced, members of BGATOS are using an Allen organ in its place. You can hear performances before each screening in the annual Summer Classics series as well as at other special screenings throughout the year.

Even without the Mighty Wurlitzer, the show goes on.

THE MIGHTY WURLITZER

WHAT: The Kentucky Theatre's organ, fully restored

WHERE: Kentucky Theatre, 214 E Main St.

COST: Ticket prices vary according to the show and screening time.

PRO TIP: Ask to speak to Fred, a legend in Lexington.

LEXINGTON SPRINGS FORTH

Where was Lexington named?

In 1750, Dr. Thomas Walker led a group into Kentucky, the first known Europeans to enter the region. Seventeen years later, Daniel Boone crossed the Cumberland Gap and led a group to central Kentucky. This started a steady influx of new arrivals including, in 1775, the McConnell brothers from Pennsylvania.

The brothers made it as far as the Elkhorn Creek. They set up a basic shelter and began mapping the area to support their land claim. Shortly afterward, they received word from Fort Boonesborough that the battle of Lexington and Concord had

MCCONNELL SPRINGS

WHAT: A 26-acre park based around a series of historic springs

WHERE: 416 Rebmann Ln.

COST: Free

PRO TIP: Pets are not allowed, even when leashed. Bicycles are also not allowed.

The Blue Hole is one of the three natural springs at McConnell Springs Park.

This bur oak was likely in its youth when the McConnells first claimed the area in 1775.

started the Revolutionary War. They decided to name their new settlement Lexington to mark the event.

Thus the future city of Lexington was named at the springs, which, in turn, were named for the McConnells. The town would receive its charter in 1782, and the rest is history. Lexington celebrated its 250th anniversary in 2025.

By the latter part of the 20th century, the area around McConnell Springs was little more than a waste dump. The city launched a plan to clean it and restore the historical site. In 1994, McConnell Springs opened as a 26-acre park.

There are several points of geological and historical significance at McConnell Springs. The titular springs are actually three natural springs: the Blue Hole, the Boils, and the Final Sink. The water flows into the sinkhole at the latter only to emerge at Preston's Cave a few miles away.

Other features in the park include the remains of the foundations for a barn and dairy and some rock wall fragments.

A bur oak within the park is believed to be between 250 and 300 years old. A crutch was installed to provide additional support for the tree in 2017.

NEXT STOP

What's the creative water reclamation system at this old bus station?

What happens when an early 20th-century building gets fitted with 21st-century know-how? A whole bunch of rainwater is stored and reused.

The innovative system at Greyline Station helps to reduce the risk of flooding while collecting, treating, and reusing rainwater in a model of sustainability.

GREYLINE STATION

WHAT: A bus station turned small business hub

WHERE: 101 W Loudon Ave.

COST: Free to browse, but take your wallet for food, wine, and more retail therapy

PRO TIP: LexTran has a direct route between Greyline and downtown.

The former bus station on Loudon Avenue was built in 1928 as the hub for Southeastern Greyhound Lines. At one time the largest private employer in the city, by 1960 it was empty. LexTran, the city's bus service, took it over for awhile, but then it stood empty again until it was bought with a plan to redevelop it as a shopping and dining hub.

While it was being renovated, the owners took the opportunity to make some eco-friendly upgrades. The roof was designed to encourage runoff into a series of gutters that feed into a system of underground pipes where the water is treated before being

---

North Lime Coffee & Donuts has been in the space since 2012, before the renovation. They offer a wide range of doughnuts (including vegan options). Maple bacon? Lavender blueberry? Turtle cheesecake? Better get a box!

A former agricultural water tank has been repurposed for rainwater storage.

fed into toilets. Additional runoff is collected through permeable surfaces in the parking lot and is then stored in a large tank for watering plants and greenspace. The system prevents waste and helps to reduce the water bills for the building's tenants. With 65,000 square feet of usable space inside Greyline, that's a lot of water that can be reused.

Inside Greyline, one section has been developed into a market kitchen, providing access to commercial equipment for food start-ups. Another area, the Clerestory, provides event space for everything from business meetings to weddings. Greyline contains a wine bar, eateries, vintage shops, and even a radio station. An interior market also offers booth space for smaller businesses. Regular evening markets are held during the holidays, and the surrounding neighborhood is being revitalized by the new traffic.

FORGOTTEN CHAMPIONS OF THE TRACK

Who were the black jockeys who shaped horse racing?

Some of the names are still familiar around town. Isaac Murphy Memorial Art Garden. Oliver Lewis Way. What is less well-known by many is the impact that they and dozens of other black horsemen had on the early days of professional racing.

Kentucky horse farms long relied on enslaved people to perform the necessary care of their animals, from basic stable care to training for races. After emancipation, many who were now free chose to continue on the farms. Without their skills and experience, the horse farms, and indeed the entire local horse industry, may well have collapsed.

Likewise, the first professional jockeys were mostly either born into slavery or born to formerly enslaved parents. Oliver Lewis, born in 1856, was one of the few born in a free family. Isaac Murphy was born into slavery in 1861, and James Perkins (born 1879) was the son of freed slaves.

Lewis, Murphy, and Perkins all went on to become champions of the racing world. Lewis won the first Kentucky Derby in 1875 on Aristides; Murphy won the Derby three times; and Perkins rode Halma to victory in the Derby in 1895.

The Isaac Murphy Memorial Art Garden stands where Murphy's house once stood. It marks the start of the Legacy Trail, a 12-mile walking and cycling path that leads to the Kentucky Horse Park.

By the time Perkins won, opportunities for black jockeys were few. White jockeys unionized in 1892 and made a concerted effort to create a color barrier in the racing world. By 1911, there were only two African American jockeys in the Derby. When Marlon St. Julien competed in the 2000 Kentucky Derby, he was the first African American to do so since 1921.

Many of those who built and dominated the thoroughbred racing world in the late 19th century were laid to rest in Lexington's African Cemetery No. 2.

THE JOCKEYS WHO SHAPED RACING

WHAT: The final resting places of Isaac Murphy, Oliver Lewis, James Perkins, and more than 170 other African Americans who helped define the horse racing world

WHERE: African Cemetery No. 2, 419 E Seventh St.

COST: Free

PRO TIP: Markers in the cemetery share the histories of jockeys, groomsmen, trainers, and farriers, as well as buffalo soldiers.

Above: *Oliver Lewis rode Aristides to victory in the first Kentucky Derby but retired at the end of the season.*

Right: *Isaac Burns Murphy's remains were reinterred next to Man o' War at the Kentucky Horse Park. Courtesy Library of Congress*

Opposite: *James Perkins was nicknamed "Soup," reportedly because he loved eating soup to keep his riding weight low.*

THE BIG CHEESE

What's to discover at this urban dairy?

Everybody knows that horses are the animal on everyone's mind in central Kentucky, but there was a time when cows were not an entirely uncommon sight in Fayette County.

Ruins of a dairy barn have been found at McConnell Springs. The Cahill Dairy Farm creamery was built at the current park's location in the early 1900s.

BOONE CREEK CREAMERY

WHAT: An urban cheesemaker

WHERE: 2416 Palumbo Dr., Ste. 110

COST: Free samples

PRO TIP: Pick up other Kentucky Proud products, including local honey, chutneys, and grains.

Also at the dawn of the 20th century, James Ben Ali Haggin took ownership of Elmendorf Farm, where, in addition to breeding racing champions, he established a state-of-the-art dairy that was reportedly one of the finest anywhere. After he died in 1914, the farm (including the dairy) was dismantled and sold off.

Fast-forward another hundred years and Ed Puterbaugh, a clinical microbiologist by training, decided he needed a new hobby. Cheesemaking seemed an ideal fit with his scientific knowledge, and in just a few years he had opened Boone Creek Creamery. When Ed passed away in 2019, Brian Taylor took over the business.

Boone Creek remains one of the few urban cheesemakers in the country without an adjoining dairy. The milk used is purchased from dairies in the region. A wide variety of cheeses are made at the Palumbo Drive facility, and visitors can watch the team make the cheese by hand before trying some samples. Boone Creek makes everything from blue cheese to Scandinavian-style grilling cheese. Then there are the more creatively named varieties—Sassy Redhead, Ginger Rogers, and Some Like It Hot, to name just a few. Fudge and butter

Top left: *A sampling of Boone Creek products. Courtesy Nic Brown*

Top right: *Boone Creek Creamery makes cheese by hand at its facility in Lexington. Courtesy Nic Brown*

Bottom: *Elmendorf's dairy was state-of-the-art. Courtesy Lexington Public Library*

are also made on-site. The cheeses are available at the creamery store, in a few local stores, and at the local farmers market.

Kentucky's not just for bourbon. Try some local cheese.

James Ben Ali Haggin made his fortune in copper and gold mining. He expanded Elmendorf to nearly 9,000 acres, with 2,000 horses, a dairy, and its own power plant.

NEW ROOTS, OLD TRADITIONS

Where can you find the freshest, most authentic tortillas in town?

The 1990 census showed 2,556 people of Hispanic origin living in Lexington. Since then, the number has increased to more than 25,000. According to the most recent census, the Hispanic population of Lexington accounts for about 9.2 percent of the city's total population.

Forty or so years ago, those who came to the area were largely migrant workers taking seasonal work on the tobacco farms. A growing number also came to work on the horse farms, and eventually families laid down roots. Today, the local Hispanic community is a vibrant mix of nationalities, all of whom are represented in the annual Festival Latino, a two-day celebration of the city's Latino culture held downtown.

One area of Lexington, Cardinal Valley, is nicknamed Mexington for its large number of Hispanic residents and businesses (although several other neighborhoods have a higher proportion of Spanish-speaking residents). The neighborhood features restaurants, bakeries, clothing stores, and other Spanish-owned businesses.

Many locals will know Ouita Michel and Jonathan Lundy, award-winning chefs. What few may realize is that there is another local award-winner on the food scene. Her name is Laura Patricia Ramírez. She came to Lexington from Guadalajara, Mexico, in 1985 with her husband and young

---

From 2001 to 2019, Lexington had its own bilingual newspaper. *La Voz* is no longer in circulation, but the archives are available for viewing at the University of Kentucky.

Left: *Corn, sourced from local farms, is ground daily to make the tortillas.*

Below: *Approximately 3,000 corn tortillas are made every morning using equipment shipped from Guadalajara.*

TORTILLERIA Y TAQUERIA RAMIREZ

WHAT: Homemade corn tortillas, freshly prepared Mexican food, and snacks

WHERE: 1429 Alexandria Dr.

COST: Prices vary for freshly made tortillas, food, and other groceries.

PRO TIP: Corn tortillas are made fresh every morning and can be purchased by the bag.

son. As the Hispanic population grew, she realized that Chicago was the nearest place to find a lot of Mexican food supplies. So she began a tortilla-making business. The store has since grown to provide an array of fresh-made food, from burritos to tortas.

In 2017, the Southern Food Alliance presented Ramírez with the Ruth Fertel Keeper of the Flame Award. The award honors someone who is maintaining food traditions and contributing to the food culture of the American South.

GRAINS, GROOVES, GALLERIES

MALT HOUSE/ DIXIELAND/LUIGART

WHAT: An example of the ingenuity in recreating space

WHERE: 110 Luigart Ct.

COST: Visit for free during the regular LexArts HOP.

PRO TIP: LuigART Studios is just a short walk from Greyline Station.

What malt warehouse became an art studio by way of a dance hall?

Lexington is an ever-changing landscape. One building that demonstrates this better than most is the Luigart Malt House, currently LuigART Studios.

The main 17,000-square-foot structure was built in the 1850s (although the listed size varies greatly in different records). Extensions were added in 1881 and 1922. Records mention a hemp factory from as early as 1834 and suggest that it was the first steam-powered hemp factory in the US. By the 1870s the building had changed hands and was being used as a malt house. Grains would have been delivered here to be prepared for use as malt in local breweries and distilleries. At this point in Lexington's history, the neighborhood around Loudon and Luigart was an industrial hub, with warehouses for receiving and shipping agricultural products.

The business was struggling by the early 1900s and the new owner, John Luigart, was keen to

Above: *During its incarnation as Dixieland Gardens, the building also housed a small hotel and a barbershop.*

Opposite: *It's had many different uses, but the exterior of the building remains largely unchanged.*

explore alternative uses for the building. In 1937 he opened part of it as Dixieland Gardens. The dance club was for local black patrons and attracted some star acts. Count Basie played there in 1940, and Ella Fitzgerald performed twice in 1941. The club received little media coverage, but it seems that by 1944, the dance hall had ceased operations.

Other businesses came and went, and the building was sold and resold. In 2017, new owners bought it with no clear idea of how to use the space. Soon artist friends asked to rent a spot, and the idea for LuigART was born. Local artists rent studio space while the upstairs is used for art shows and other events.

The building has its groove back.

In 1943, a disgruntled white bus driver fired into Dixieland Gardens, killing a white student and injuring two young African American men. He was sentenced to two years in prison but was released after six months.

Ginkgo, *a stainless steel sculpture by Warren Seelig, stands in the Rotunda of the Albert B. Chandler Hospital. Courtesy UK Arts in HealthCare*

SOURCES

I Dream of Monkeys
visitlex.com/things-to-do/all-attractions/mural-challenge

findmasa.com/artist/herakut

fairytalenewsblog.blogspot.com/2013/06/herakut-my-what-big-tales-you-have.html

urban-nation.com/artist/herakut

Mysterious Mounds
sah-archipedia.org/buildings/KY-01-067-0057

onlyinyourstate.com/experiences/kentucky/destination-that-baffles-archaeologists-ky

archaeology.ky.gov/Find-a-Site/Pages/Mt.-Horeb.aspx

megalithic.co.uk/article.php?sid=57442

heritage.ky.gov/archaeology/prehistoric/Pages/Paleoindian.aspx#:~:text=Sites%20found%20in%20Kentucky%20are,sites%20are%20rare%20in%20Kentucky

Building a Fairytale
thekentuckycastle.com

firehouse.com/home/news/10530945/kentucky-castle-fire-likely-arson

architecturaldigest.com/gallery/most-beautiful-hotels-in-america

architecturaldigest.com/gallery/worlds-most-luxurious-castles-sleep-in

Big Blue
skyscrapercenter.com/building/lexington-financial-center/9470

thewebbcompanies.com/2017/12/19/lexington-financial-center

loc.gov/resource/highsm.63781

kentucky.com/news/local/article44399496.html

kentucky.com/living/article44445537.html

Go Medieval
airbnb.com/rooms/38573040

Raise a Glass
constitutionbookstore.com

kentucky.com/lexgoeat/bourbon/article284859001.html

Bring the Jelly
jif.com/our-history

kentucky.com/news/local/counties/fayette-county/article261705997.html

fox56news.com/news/local/10-facts-about-kentuckys-own-jif-peanut-butter

nationalpeanutboard.org/news/fun-facts

A Political Hairball
libguides.transy.edu/aboutspec/MoosnickMuseum

kyhi.org/transylvania-university-medical-department

Play Ball
facebook.com/profile.php?id=100057323775500

winchestersun.com/2021/05/07/the-old-ball-game-bluegrass-barons-play-base-ball-1869-style/

courier-journal.com/story/news/local/2019/10/30/bluegrass-barons-vintage-baseball-team-kentucky/3987628002/

youtube.com/watch?v=Lwufr7ikn7Q

britannica.com/topic/Major-League-Baseball

Hail the King
Foody, Terry. *The Pie Seller, the Drunk, and the Lady.* Terry Foody, 2014.

jpinews.com/2017/09/01/my-kentucky-solomon-and-charlotte-an-unlikely-partnership

The Mostest Hoss
man-owar.com

web.archive.org/web/20170330010526/http://www.horsemanmagazine.com/2009/07/the-story-of-man-o-war

racingmuseum.org/hall-of-fame/horse/man-o-war-ky

kyhorsepark.com/explore/man-o-war

Roots of History
floracliff.org

floracliff.org/the-sanctuary/floracliffs-old-trees-rays-of-hope-for-the-inner-bluegrass-region

knps.org/from-the-lady-slipper-archive-floracliffs-old-trees

Sins of the Past
loc.gov/item/2003669659

visitlex.com/listing/henry-a-tandy-centennial-park/7326

history.ky.gov/markers/cheapside-slave-auction-block

lexingtonhistory.wordpress.com/2009/05/23/cheapside-more-than-a-name

kentucky.com/news/local/counties/fayette-county/article245309985.html

blackpast.org/african-american-history/tandy-vertner-woodson-1885-1949

Cures and Cocktails
atlasobscura.com/places/bondurants-pharmacy

kentucky.com/news/business/article44097537.html

designingbuildings.co.uk/wiki/Mimetic_architecture

Ginkgo Gold
lextoday.6amcity.com/catalpa-roads-gingko-trees-brings-a-tunnel-of-gold-to-chevy-chase

visitlex.com/guides/post/fall-foliage-in-lexington

lex18.com/news/covering-kentucky/lexington-cemetery-cherry-blossoms-make-their-return

Cross the River
lextoday.6amcity.com/valley-view-ferry-lexington-ky

lexingtonky.gov/valley-view-ferry

noclexington.com/valley-view-a-ferry-history

madisonsheritage.eku.edu/items/show/636

UFO Landing
winchestersun.com/2017/04/14/charles-mitchell-the-coca-cola-man

web.commercelexington.com/Beverage-Dist-Bottlers/CocaCola-Consolidated-Inc-241

visitlex.com/aliens

KnowhutImean?
atlasobscura.com/places/jim-varney-grave

smileypete.com/community/2014-01-16-jim-varney-biography-traces-the-cultural-rise-of-ernest-p-worrell

imdb.com/name/nm0001815/?ref_=hm_rvi_i_1

Reviving a Lost Craft
drystone.org

hmdb.org/m.asp?m=194586

wkyt.com/2024/10/11/saving-kentuckys-stone-fences

kentucky.com/news/local/counties/fayette-county/article296104954.html

kentucky.com/news/local/counties/bourbon-county/article44492352.html

A Late One
Young-Brown, Fiona. *A Culinary History of Kentucky: Burgoo, Beer Cheese, and Goetta.* The History Press, 2014.

ale8one.com

Phantoms' Watch
lexingtonky.gov/government/departments-programs/public-safety/fire-emergency-services/fire-station-locations

kentucky.com/news/local/counties/fayette-county/article158478874.html

southernspiritguide.org/firehouse-phantom-lexington-kentucky

northsidelex.com/imagevault/f1367946699.pdf

Drink Up
dixie.com/about

atlasobscura.com/places/dixie-cup-water-tower

kentucky.com/news/business/article248529340.html

news.gp.com/2020/11/georgia-pacific-completes-100-million-expansion-of-bowling-green-dixie-facility

Swing Time
britannica.com/science/Foucault-pendulum

worldrecordacademy.org/2023/9/worlds-largest-ceiling-clock-world-record-in-lexington-kentucky-423371

lexpublib.org/locations/central-library

libguides.uky.edu/LittleLibraryart/adalin-wichman

lunamosaicarts.com/blogs/featured-artist-of-the-month/terri-pulley

guinnessworldrecords.com/world-records/largest-pendulum-regulated-clock

web.archive.org/web/20161106062451

www.kentuckystewarts.com/RowanCounty/LucilleCaudill.htm

The Final Stretch
tbheritage.com/TurfHallmarks/Graves/cem/GraveMattersHamburg.html

theriverbendgroup.com/what-is-legacy

A Genteel Pastime
parks.ky.gov/explore/waveland-state-historic-site-7805

visitlex.com/listing/waveland-state-historic-site/5915

www.heritagehemptrail.com

kentuckyhistorictravels.com/2024/06/29/waveland-historic-site-exploring-the-fascinating-boone-bryan-history

From Bridles to Brides
onlyinyourstate.com/experiences/kentucky/round-barn-stable-ky

npgallery.nps.gov/NRHP/GetAsset/NRHP/77000612_text

visitlex.com/listing/the-round-barn-stable-of-memories/7161

bayoubluegrass.com

harnesslink.com/usa/for-immediate-release-brittany-trophies-to-stable-of-memories

Rebuilding a Revolutionary Bourbon
jamesepepper.com

jamesepepper.com/pepper-history

Taking a Bite out of Learning
transy.edu/about/who-we-are/our-history

transy.edu/about/who-we-are/quick-facts

Baffling Burials
transyrambler.com/2016/10/25/who-is-rafinesque

libguides.transy.edu/SpecialCollections/RafinesqueBotanicGarden

lewis-clark.org/people/constantine-rafinesque

transy.edu/1780/2019/09/honor-to-whom-honor-is-overdue-transylvania-remembers-noted-professor-constantine-rafinesque

transy.edu/1780/2023/10/transylvania-community-celebrates-rafs-240th-birthday

Tracing the Lineage
martinabros.com/case-studies/blue-grass-airport

bluegrassairport.com

prominentsirelines.com

visitlex.com/things-to-do/horses/horse-farm-tours

The Final Resting Place of Madam Belle
content.time.com/time/subscriber/article/0,33009,764506,00.html

kentuckymonthly.com/belle-brezing

uknow.uky.edu/campus-news/book-sheds-new-light-infamous-lexington-madam

Dueling Doctors
Young-Brown, Fiona. *Wicked Lexington, Kentucky*. The History Press, 2011.

kentucky.com/entertainment/visual-arts/article44567064.html

wuky.org/wuky-in-depth/2019-09-14/not-even-the-end-of-the-civil-war-could-stop-men-of-honor-from-dueling-in-kentucky

kentucky.com/news/state/kentucky/article231254993.html

loc.gov/item/2010717062

Showing the Way
kentucky.com/news/know-your-kentucky/article288996879.html

explorelexingtonky.com/blog/lexington-ky-is-known-for-its-famous-race-horses-and-its-camel-statue

The Forgotten Novelist
carnegiecenterlex.org/hall-of-fame/james-lane-allen

hmdb.org/m.asp?m=59083

gratzpark.org/?page_id=137

roadsideamerica.com/tip/60825

nytimes.com/1954/12/14/archives/joseph-p-pollia.html

Lucky Lindy's Lex
explorekyhistory.ky.gov/items/show/708

history.ky.gov/markers/lexingtons-first-airport

kentucky.com/news/local/counties/fayette-county/article44525766.html

aviationky.org

postalmuseum.si.edu/exhibition/fad-to-fundamental-airmail-in-america-airmail-pilot-stories-contract-pilots/charles#:~:text=Lindbergh

Lights, Camera, Lexington
lexstudios.tv

kentuckymonthly.com/explore/places/hooray-for-lexington

lanereport.com/49980/2015/06/kentucky-improves-film-and-tv-incentives

Remembering the 49
kentucky.com/news/special-reports/crash-of-comair-flight-5191/article44092662.html

kentucky.com/news/special-reports/crash-of-comair-flight-5191/article44035002.html

kentucky.com/news/local/counties/fayette-county/article98346097.html

douwestudios.com

arboretum.ca.uky.edu

A Literary Pig

kentucky.com/news/local/counties/fayette-county/article86107512.html

riversidefoodtours.com/cincinnatis-love-affair-with-pigs

365cincinnati.com/big-pig-gig

facesandplaces.kentonlibrary.org/index.php?-q=aerial+view+cincinnati&s=false&p=32

kentucky.com/entertainment/visual-arts/article44567064.html

Old Spice

lexhistory.org/wp-content/uploads/2022/05/LexHist-NewsletterSpringE.pdf

sites.rootsweb.com/~kyfayett/inventions.htm

hmdb.org/m.asp?m=169860

kentucky.com/news/local/article281946448.html

hollyhillandco.com/shop/p/wallace-station-bourbon-mustard

Time Keeps Ticking

hmdb.org/m.asp?m=119118

wkyt.com/2023/10/10/historic-downtown-lexington-landmark-removed-after-damage

kentucky.com/news/local/counties/fayette-county/article44444385.html

Stranger Than Fiction

kyforky.com/blogs/journal/cocaine-bear

courier-journal.com/story/money/louisville-city-living/2021/03/11/kentucky-cocaine-bear-legend-subject-of-movie-by-elizabeth-banks/4830810002

wsj.com/articles/cocaine-bear-true-story-movie-lexington-kentucky-94aadc1c

vanityfair.com/hollywood/2023/02/the-real-cocaine-bear

vanityfair.com/hollywood/2023/02/cocaine-bear-true-story

A Forgotten Place

kentucky.com/news/health-and-medicine/article44607351.html

findagrave.com/cemetery/2233199/memorial-search?cemeteryName=Hull-Mc Gowan+Cemetery&page=1#sr-46803959

newspapers.com/article/lexington-herald-leader/133500939

youtube.com/watch?v=ccvx6-hrloA

ites.rootsweb.com/~kycampbe/piecesjohncampbell.htm

Round and Round

wellingtonparklabyrinth.wordpress.com

lextoday.6amcity.com/wellington-park-labyrinth-lexington-kentucky

artemisinitiative.org/blank-1

hunterlex.org

The Secret Garden

exploreuk.uky.edu/fa/findingaid/?id=xt76q52f925g

gardenstogables.com/photosynthesis-for-the-soul-the-mathews-garden-at-the-university-of-kentucky

Eblen, Tom. "UK should reconsider demolishing historic lab." *Lexington Herald-Leader*, April 23, 2014, A3.

kentucky.com/opinion/op-ed/article59399803.html

Reece, Erik. "Save golden glory of 660 - biophilia thrives in wild of UK's Mathews Garden." *Lexington Herald-Leader*, May 4, 2014, E1.

Mad or Misunderstood

Baker, Jean H. *Mary Todd Lincoln: A Biography*. Norton, 1987.

mtlhouse.org

apps.legislature.ky.gov/LegislativeMoments/moments08RS/21_web_leg_moments.htm

explorekyhistory.ky.gov/items/show/129

Evolution

player.vimeo.com/video/111310990

urbanllama.com/2015/03/09/mural-by-mto-adds-intrigue-to-manchester-street-in-lexington

brooklynstreetart.com/2014/11/20/fighting-prohibition-with-mto-in-lexington-ky

kentucky.com/living/article44517609.html

Shaping the Past, Shaping the Future

lexingtonhamlets.org

heritage.ky.gov/Documents/RosenwaldSchoolsinKY.pdf

npgallery.nps.gov/NRHP/GetAsset/NRHP/06000213_text

lexingtonky.news/2023/04/08/a-one-room-schoolhouse-with-a-powerful-history-effort-underway-to-preserve-fayette-countys-rosenwald-school

nkaa.uky.edu/nkaa/items/show/1472

Tales of a Talking Tree
howardcurry.com

facebook.com/lexhistory/posts/1094367316035163

smileypete.com/business/corman-and-associates

cormanmarketplace.com

Where Christmas Shines Bright
wkyt.com/2022/12/01/lexington-christmas-house-shines-bright-this-holiday-season

kentucky.com/news/local/counties/fayette-county/article43975140.html

kentucky.com/news/local/counties/fayette-county/article44016972.html

kentucky.com/news/local/counties/fayette-county/article44391579.html

lextoday.6amcity.com/christmas-lights-in-lexington-ky

Art of Contention
kentucky.com/news/local/education/article286822285.html

kentucky.com/news/local/education/article269076877.html

uky.edu/prmarketing/memorial-hall-mural

ohanloncenter.org/about/story/the-ann-ohanlon-story

ohanloncenter.org/wp-content/uploads/2020/07/Opinion-by-Karyn-Olivier-on-OH-mural.pdf

kentucky.com/news/local/education/article216588570.html

britannica.com/topic/Public-Works-of-Art-Project

libguides.uky.edu/AnnRiceOHanlon/MIKMurals

Poor Boy Blues
kentucky.com/lexgoeat/restaurants/article262981153.html

smileypete.com/business/2012-03-02-parkette-drive-in-history-isnt-just-leftovers

smileypete.com/business/2012-03-02-renovated-parkette-seeks-more-nostalgia-than-just-its-look

foodnetwork.com/restaurants/ky/lexington/parkette-drive-in-restaurant

Full Steam Ahead
sites.rootsweb.com/~kyfayett/inventions.htm

filsonhistorical.org/wp-content/uploads/publicationpdfs/21-4-4_Edward-West-Silversmith-and-Inventor_Bridwell-Margaret-M..pdf

lextoday.6amcity.com/steamboat-invented-lexington-kentucky-1793

hmdb.org/m.asp?m=58557

datamp.org/patents/advance.php?pn=381X&id=18059&set=36

invent.org/inductees/john-fitch

apps.legislature.ky.gov/LegislativeMoments/Moments21RS/web/legmo_10.pdf

Mobile Home
daytonhistorybooks.com/page/page/1571350.htm

samterryskentucky.com/kentucky-history/f/pattersons-cabin-in-the-athens-of-the-west

daytonpioneers.org/the-pioneers/patterson-family

daytonpioneers.org/the-pioneers/brown-family

A Modernist Masterpiece
voices.uchicago.edu/201504arth15709-01a2/2015/11/16/le-corbusier

archpaper.com/2021/05/two-historic-homes-in-lexington-kentucky-face-potential-demolition

matthagen.org/blog/lexington-modern-the-miller-house

themillerhouseky.com

world-architects.com/en/architecture-news/headlines/jose-oubrerie-1932-2024

sitelecorbusier.com/en/discover/church-of-saint-pierre

Spam and *Pulp Fiction*
bigkahunalex.com

kentucky.com/lexgoeat/restaurants/article250171515.html

kentucky.com/lexgoeat/restaurants/article295606539.html

North to Freedom
freedomcenter.org/heroes/lewis-hayden

nps.gov/boaf/learn/historyculture/lewis-and-harriet-hayden-house.htm

lexfreedomtrain.org

visitlex.com/guides/post/underground-railroad-stop

https://spame.org

Creating a Waterfront
kelleyslanding.com

kentucky.com/news/local/counties/fayette-county/article288163875.html

spectrumnews1.com/ky/louisville/news/2024/05/01/kelley-s-landing-lexington

Roots and Resistance
nkaa.uky.edu/nkaa/items/show/333

kentucky.com/news/local/counties/fayette-county/article291175935.html

segregatedlexington.com/urban-renewal

Heart of the East End
historiclyrictheatre.com

cvky.org/brightening-our-future-embracing-our-past

smileypete.com/business/2012-03-02-celebrating-the-lyric

historiclyrictheatre.com/2023/12/08/elementor-937

tourthehistoricbluegrass.com/tours/show/1

Greens and Fins
foodchainlex.org/aquaponics-farm

kentucky.com/lexgoeat/food/article239274998.html

smithtownseafood.com

westsixth.com

windycornermarket.com/chef-ouitas-family-of-restaurants

Good Boy
smileypete.com/smiley-petes-story

lextoday.6amcity.com/smiley-pete-town-dog-lexington-ky

A Hole-y Experience
lexingtonicecenter.com/about-miniature-golf

atlasobscura.com/places/lexington-s-biblical-miniature-golf

theguardian.com/travel/shortcuts/2019/jul/30/holey-moly-the-worlds-ten-most-sensational-minigolf-courses

The Healing Power of Art
ukhealthcare.uky.edu/arts-in-healthcare

ukhealthcare.uky.edu/arts-in-healthcare/visual-arts/rotating-galleries

cvky.org/uk-arts-in-healthcare-art-inc-kentucky-brings-healing-to-patients-through-art

ukhealthcare.uky.edu/sites/default/files/self-guided-art-tour.pdf

Totally in Love
21cmuseumhotels.com/museum/exhibit/totally-in-love/?ipid=il

kentucky.com/news/know-your-kentucky/article299378314.html

21cmuseumhotels.com/nightwatch

21cmuseumhotels.com/lexington

Caves of Crystals and Mummies
uky.edu/OtherOrgs/KPS/books/funkwebb/funkwebbch06.pdf

uky.edu/KGS/geoky/county/fayette.htm

chicagotribune.com/2004/05/29/developer-gets-approval-to-build-houses-above-cave

city-data.com/forum/lexington-area/1507419-cave-off-russel-cave-road.html#google_vignette

hmdb.org/m.asp?m=194584

vulcanmaterials.com

Fun Divided
explorekyhistory.ky.gov/items/show/870

history.ky.gov/markers/joyland-amusement-park

Ruins Among the Roots
ravenrun.org

eec.ky.gov/Nature-Preserves/Locations/Pages/Raven-Run.aspx

Ku, Michelle. "Lexington seeks ideas for saving historic farmhouse." *Lexington Herald-Leader (KY)*, November 10, 2004: C3.

Dottie Bean. "The expansion of raven run sanctuary grows with popularity." *Lexington Herald-Leader (KY)*, July 12, 1990: B1.

kentuckykindredgenealogy.com/2017/04/28/fayette-countys-raven-run-nature-sanctuary-and-a-genealogy-discovery

Wrapped in Gold
kentucky.com/entertainment/visual-arts/article44040252.html

kentucky.com/entertainment/visual-arts/article44066934.html

jamesherman.net/galleries4/eastern-time/lexington-horses-2000

thegrovelex.com

npgallery.nps.gov/NRHP/GetAsset/NRHP/73000799_text

Timeless Magic
themagicclockshop.com

smileypete.com/arts-and-culture/2012-03-02-the-clock-shop

studios180.com/5-unique-shops-in-around-downtown-lexington

Reborn from the Ashes, and Repeat
theclio.com/entry/88539

theclio.com/entry/45856

kentucky.com/news/know-your-kentucky/article301885789.html

facebook.com/100063857143330/posts/1124725982999296/?_rdr

sites.rootsweb.com/~kyfayett/dunn/keiser_benj.htm

A Museum of Gems and Shells
headley-whitney.org

kentucky.com/entertainment/visual-arts/article44399658.html

keeneland.com/sites/default/files/PolishingAJewel.pdf

en.chateauversailles.fr/discover/estate/gardens/groves

Hidden but Revealed
gattonpark.org

smileypete.com/community/2012-04-14-a-creek-runs-under-it

history.ky.gov/markers/town-branch

townbranch.org/tbww/history.html

lexingtonky.gov/government/mayors-office/town-branch-commons

uky-gis.github.io/maps/lex-tbt-main-st

Bohemian Sanctuary
smileypete.com/business/2013-05-30-restoration-breathes-new-life-and-historic-character-into-former-home-of-local-artist-henry-faulkner

kentucky.com/living/home-garden/article44423421.html

Robots and Ramen
pressroom.toyota.com/facility/toyota-motor-manufacturing-kentucky

kentucky.com/news/business/article285106817.html

zundolexington.com

lexingtonsistercities.org/shinhidaka%2C-japan

Magic Pat-land
thirdststuff.com

kentucky.com/living/article88870837.html

smileypete.com/community/creative-types-pat-gerhard

businessinsider.com/best-coffee-shops-in-the-us-2014-7

Where Mental Health Care Began
kyhi.org/asylums/eastern-state-hospital

asylumprojects.org/index.php?title=Eastern_State_Hospital_Lexington

history.ky.gov/markers/eastern-state-hospital

hazlitt.net/feature/such-laugh-one-might-fancy-satan-uttered

bluegrass.kctcs.edu/about/campuses/newtown

Still Keeping House
gratzpark.org/?page_id=90

keeneland.com/sites/default/files/BodleyBullockHouse.pdf

southernspiritguide.org/old-morrison-and-the-gratz-park-historic-district

bluegrasswinners.com/about-us

lexarts.org/discover/lexarts-hop

Echoes of the Silver Screen
kentuckytheatre.org

dosvatos.com/TheKentuckyTheatre/history.htm

kentucky.com/living/article90255362.html

bgatos.org/the-wurlitzer

kentucky.com/opinion/linda-blackford/article265666101.html

smileypete.com/arts-and-culture/2012-03-02-the-heart-of-the-kentucky-theatre

Lexington Springs Forth
mcconnellsprings.org

lexingtonky.gov/playing/parks-natural-areas/natural-areas/mcconnell-springs-park

hmdb.org/m.asp?m=194587

hmdb.org/m.asp?m=194585

hmdb.org/m.asp?m=194583

Next Stop
informedinfrastructure.com/71493/from-bus-repairs-to-water-reclaimation-old-kentucky-building-brings-new-uses-for-storm-runoff

greylinestation.com

smileypete.com/community/market-day-greyline-station-prepares-to-open

northlime.net

Forgotten Champions of the Track

hmdb.org/m.asp?m=119101

hmdb.org/m.asp?m=119099

hmdb.org/m.asp?m=202886

hmdb.org/m.asp?m=202887

africancemeteryno2.org

businessinsider.com/why-black-jockeys-disappeared-from-the-kentucky-derby-2022-5

The Big Cheese

paulickreport.com/news/bloodstock/kentucky-farm-time-capsule-elmendorf-farm

stonecolumnsstables.com/history-of-elmendorf-farm

boonecreekcreamery.com

hungrytravelers.com/boone-creek-creamery-makes-real-ky-cheese

kentuckyliving.com/lifestyle/kentucky-says-cheese

New Roots, Old Traditions

kentucky.com/news/local/counties/fayette-county/article277626973.html

kentucky.com/news/local/counties/fayette-county/article253454799.html

southernfoodways.org/film/mexington

southernfoodways.org/awards/2017-ruth-fertel-keeper-of-the-flame-laura-patricia-ramirez

libraries.uky.edu/news/keeping-la-voz-alive-uk-libraries-preserves-unique-bilingual-paper-documenting-growth

Grains, Grooves, Galleries

heritage.ky.gov/Documents/Fayette%20County,%20Luigart%20Malt%20House,%20final.pdf

nkaa.uky.edu/nkaa/items/show/300004298

kyphotoarchive.com/2018/02/12/dixieland-gardens-shooting-scene-1943

smileypete.com/community/luigart-studios-communal-creativity

facebook.com/Luigartstudios

INDEX

The site of the old Evans Mill is also within Raven Run's boundaries. Courtesy Patrick Jennings